My W.C. Fields

My Walnut Creek and the Southside Gang

By Albert Don Henderson

Copyright ©2017, Albert D Henderson

No part of this publication may be reproduced, stored in retrieval system, or transmitted in any form by any means without prior written permission of the publisher.

All Rights Reserved

Dedicated to My Lifelong Friend, Eddie Nokes

And to all the great memories we shared as Southside members

Remembering my good friend Royce Shelton for

"Another fine mess you got me into."

Contents

My W.C. Fields Introduction By A. D. Henderson 7
The Southside Gang 11
My Early Football 15
My Football Injuries and other stories 24
Nicknames 28
Stepping Down From the Train 30
Remembering Christmas Neighbors 33
    Christmas Fireworks 39
Ice cream 42
Sugar Sack 44
My Connections with Royce 45
Sammy Shelton 47
Rooster Dodson 50
DUMB BUM 55
Jeep, Jack Rabbits, and Juice 57
Hay Hauling 59
Watermelons 62
Chinaberry Fights 64
Corn Cob Fights 66
Mud Ball Fights 70
Rubber Gun Fights 73
Sling Shots 75
Killing Birds 77
Dove Hunting 82
Ducks 85

Crows and Banty Hens	86
Dynamite	88
The Inch Pond	92
Tops and School Yard Games	95
ODE TO EDDIE'S TOP	99
Apple Core, Apple Core, Who's Your Friends	100
School Pranks	102
The Board of Education	106
My 39 Chevy Coup	109
My Aggie Trip with Royce	115
This was the AGGIE VARSITY roster for 1956.	120
My Student Council Tenure	123
Golden Gloves 1957	127
After The '55 Team, Nokes No Joke	141
My Rendition of	143
NOKES NO JOKE	144
GOOD DEFENDERS	145
Royce and Golf	147
Clouds and Temptations	148
Eddie's Temptation	148
Eddie's New Rod and Reel	149
Grappling by Grandpa	151
Raising Rabbits	152
Easter Chickens	155
COAL OIL RAGS AND CASTER OIL	157
Sitting On the North Pole	161
Nokes Yard Games	167

The Thing	168
Sand Games	170
Television in the 40's and 50's	173
Stilts, Cans and Paddle Ball	176
Kites, Gliders and Parachutes	180
Willie Romine	185
Dodd's Lake	188
The Dodd's Skating Rink	191
Four and Twenty Blackbirds	193
Comic Books	194
Wheaties and Post Toasties	195
My Grandmother's Nose	196
Polk Salad	196
Golfing with the Farrells	198
Ode to Uncle Frank	199
OUR LIFE IS LIKE A TREE	203
THE OLD ROCK SCHOOL	205
Last Run to Glory	207
POSTSCRIPT 12/30/2022	210
He's In God's Hands	211
Thank you, God, for protecting us all those years from ourselves	211
Albert D. Henderson's "Other Books":	212

My W.C. Fields Introduction By A. D. Henderson

No, not W.C. Fields the actor. My W.C. is "Walnut Creek," a small little creek in Henderson County (No kin to me that I know), near Malakoff, Texas. Some of my earliest and best memories are supplied by that small body of water. Eddie Nokes, (My next-door neighbor, my high school chum and best friend), Royce Shelton, Sammy Shelton, Gordon Lynne (Rooster) Dodson, Paul Davis (P.D.) Bankston and I would roam the W.C. woods, swinging on grape vines, fishing, running around and hunting for any wild animal that moved. I believe that all people and events will live, as long as we remember them, so that is what I am trying to do. REMEMBER THEM!! At one time Walton Creek must have been a tributary of The Trinity River, although I've never researched it. (Maybe I should) Walnut Creek wound through several properties on which we often roamed sunup to sundown. The good thing in those days, we were safe; well, kind of. We were never safe from Royce Shelton's eager mind. He was always plotting some new venture for us to get into. As an example, the time he talked the Southside group into having a BB gun fight. I had my Daisy pump which held 50 shots and I was a good shot with it. I usually used my BB gun for more constructive things, like killing birds. (But that's another story) Anyhow, back then we all wore blue jeans, and the rules of the game were simple: shoot below the waist only. It would sting your leg, but nothing more. In theory this was good, but when Eddie Nokes comes charging at you with his lever action daisy spraying BBs all over the place, in your excitement you may aim a little bit too high, which one day I did. Of course, Royce always organized us into teams.

Most of the time, I was on Royce's team, which usually was a good thing. One day when Eddie charged, firing from the hip, I too fired. He dropped like a big tree and lay motionless. I thought I had killed him. The things that were going through my mind; Yea, right, Royce, you said no one can get hurt. How will I explain this to his parents and to my Grandmother? What if I put his eye out? Time passed like syrup pouring off a biscuit. Then he moved. Thank, God!! He's alive!! Royce was already laughing as he usually did when one of us suffered minor misery. I don't know where P.D. (Paul Davis) was on this day, but he would have been laughing too. This ended our BB gun fights that day and forever, at least for me. God was taking care of us again. As it turned out, Eddie was hit squarely between the eyes and had a big knot there, but no permanent damage. I felt like getting down on my knees and thanking God, but I remained standing, knees shaking, and prayed silently. This battle raged in Robertson's field, one of the main properties along Walnut Creek. This field was directly behind Miss Willie West's house (I'll talk later about Miss Willie). Witt Robertson lived down the street on the way to town; north of my Grandparent's house, which was located on the Crossroads highway. It was Mr. Robertson's property where we played and crossed to get to the "creek," as we called it. Walnut Creek was about a mile southeast of Robertson's field and then wound back west toward the Crossroads highway through Ferris Shepherd's property. There on the highway a bridge crossed the creek. Another fine way Royce used the W.C; to train us for running. This happened later when we were in high school. Royce would badger us to race him to the bridge. For me it was no different than racing a horse. Eddie could stay up with him, but not me. The other rule (Royce always set the rules) … you MUST wear brogans or combat boots. This was supposed to get you in shape (or kill you). Royce's house was just south of our house, with the Dodson's home in between. The W.C. Bridge was exactly one mile from the foot of the end of Royce's driveway. Royce's house set up on top of the hill on the East side of the highway. The reason we knew it was one mile is because Royce used one of his Dad's cars to measure it. He had his choice of several cars at the time because, I.V., Royce's dad was a part time car salesman, He would buy cars at some auction in Dallas and then use the car until he sold it. Neither Eddie nor I had a car at the time, but later I'll tell you some stories about my Blue Buzzard (1939 Chevy). Of course, the race to the W.C. Bridge was always won by Royce, who not only ran like a Greek God, but he also looked like one. Me, I weighed about…well, put it this way, I may have been Outweighed by the brogans. Royce would kid me about my physic. He said, "Don you'd have run around in a shower to get wet." Eddie's only problem, well, how else can I say it? He was not inspired to run as fast as he could (lazy shouldn't be used. should it?) Eddie was as strong as an ox and pretty fast when he wanted to be. He was the calmest person I have ever known. I take that back. I saw him mad twice. Once when we were juniors, Coach Loggins kept insisting that Eddie be more aggressive. Royce was either blocking while coming through the line, or carrying the ball, and Eddie was playing defense. Royce, wanting to give Eddie a little extra incentive to be more aggressive, gave him a forearm shiver right across his throat. There was no such thing as the Incredible Hulk then, but adrenaline must have transformed Eddie into something like the hulk. He all of a sudden was a raving maniac. He saw red. The next time Royce came through the line, Eddie slammed him to the ground like he was a rag doll. Royce grinned and laughed a little, sheepishly, but he understood that he had awakened a sleeping giant and decided that he would let him sleep from then on. Royce never tried that again. The other time I saw Eddie mad was when we were Malakoff High School Seniors. Eddie was always a procrastinator when it came to homework and his senior year was no different, only worse. We all had Senioritis. We were required to do a term paper for English in order to pass our senior year. Ben Garcia and I had already done ours because we all had library (study (a joke) hall) first period and we used our time to knock out the term paper; meantime Eddie Nukes procrastinated. It was coming down to the wire, so Eddie was frantically writing away one day during study hall. Ben and I decided to grab his paper and run with it. That was a wrong move. I grabbed it and handed it to Ben and then Eddie turned into the Incredible Hulk again!! He torn out after Ben and caught him in about two bounds, twisting his arm until he dropped the papers; meantime, Eddie reached back and grabbed me. This quiet, reserve human was now a raging animal. No one was hurt, but we understood. Don't mess with Eddie's paper.

These are just a few of the exploits of our Southside gang along Walnut Creek during the late 40's and 50's and early 60's. All I can say is, "God and his angels were with us; otherwise, I would not have survived to write this!!"

The Southside Gang

Describing the Southside Gang is best done by comparing us to Spanky and the Little Rascals. We were a mischievous lot, but never harmful (at least not on purpose); nor were we dishonest (we didn't steal unless you count the watermelons or the Dynamite (another story). Our main goal was playing some game and having fun, or as we grew older, hunting and fishing. Of course, Royce always made a game out of everything we did. We were free to roam about the countryside, mostly on the South end of Malakoff, a rural community in Henderson County. All of this took place in late forties, fifties and early 60's. To be a member of the Southside gang, one had to live south of the railroad. It wasn't that we didn't admit anyone else; it was just that most of the time our games seemed to originate with those in our immediate area. There were a few who crossed over, but not that many. Since the entire town barely contained a thousand people, membership was limited. Some even said that the population of Malakoff, which was given on the road sign as 1,286, included those in the cemetery! To give you an idea of the downtown activity, when darkness fell, they rolled up the sidewalks; meaning, you couldn't find anything to do. This is when our leader, Royce, began wandering to the big city of Athens, and this is where the Southside gang often strayed after we reached high school. Names included to be written about later: Royce, Eddie, Don, Gordon Lynne (Rooster) Dodson, Sammy Shelton, Thesea Shelton, Delores (Lokie) Nokes, Sallye Dodson, Tom Billy Dodson, Delores McClain, Don McClain, Manny Day, Donnie Robertson, Paul Davis (P.D.) Bankston, Billy Joe (Toothpick) Robertson, Patsy Nokes, Kenneth Willingham, Wiley, Henry, Jimmy Allen, and Glen (Coal Oil) Johnson.

There was no doubt about who the leader was. Hands down it was Royce Wayne Shelton. Since my best memories of Royce are when he was in high school, that's the description I will give. Royce was a muscular six foot and weighed about 170 as a senior. He was narrow at the waist with wide shoulders. He could have been a model for Charles Atlas (Ok you youngsters don't know who that is. Let's just say "muscle-builder") His blond hair was either cropped short or in a flat top. His skin was a golden tan. He and I were the same age, but he outweighed me by least 50 lbs. or more. He was always one of the fastest in our group. He later became "the fastest" after he surpassed Kenneth Willingham. His senior year he ran a 10 flat 100-yard dash, which was one of the fastest in the state. Of course, this was before any of the African Americans were timed and before the run changed to meters. From his Mother he received a number of Indian traits like his dark skin, muscular build and sparse beard. I think maybe his Dad also had some Indian blood and this was genetically passed to Royce. By the time he was a senior in high school, he was an outstanding athlete, participating in football, track, and basketball. He was one of the best at anything he tried and of course in our Southside circle of friends, he was alpha dog. Though he was always dominating among our group, he was never overbearing. If he chose to, he could have crushed any one of us. Later Eddie might have stood up to him in strength but chose not to. Though we didn't "elect" Royce as our leader, he was indeed our unanimous unelected choice. With this in mind, understand that when a game or a work project or a trip was begun, Royce was behind it in one way or the other. Over the years we developed Southside Gang traits and customs. When Royce wanted us for some game get-to-gather, he would simply yell for us, and we would respond. This was in the early days before we began communicating with our "Tarzan" calls. My best friend, Eddie Nokes, lived next door to me, while Rooster lived across the street. Farther south on the east side up on the hill is where Royce, Sammy and Thesea resided. I think Eddie and I dreamed up the "Tarzan" call to signal when we wanted to alert fellow members that a "function" was eminent or to let them know we were home. As best I can remember, after seeing a Tarzan movie, Eddie and I began practicing our version of the "Tarzan" call. We found that our call could reach all the way to the Shelton's which was a good quarter mile away. If I gave a Tarzan yell and anyone heard it, within a few minutes I would get a "Tarzan" call reply. It might come from Eddie next door or Rooster across the street, and maybe even from the Shelton's hill. This was a neat way of letting each other know we were home and available for play. Other times, Royce, who had a car, would come by and honk and holler for us to come out. This usually meant going up to the high school to play football or sneaking in the gym for basketball. Many times, Royce would show up with a basketball and we knew that he was ready to play. We had an outside basketball hoop, but Royce preferred the Malakoff Gym (especially in bad weather), which was locked during "after school" hours. The trick was to scale the side of the gym and find an open window. From there it was simple. After sliding through the window, we would play for hours. Other times we would join him for a "work-detail" This was after we were older and too "mature" for rubber guns, corn cobs, mud balls or BB guns. Royce thrived on competition of some sort and early on he revved up our competitive juices. Even to this day, I enjoy competing and I believe those early days with Royce and the Southside Gang instilled this in me. Today I love Tennis competition, which; by the way, was one of the few games I could beat Royce. Royce was the Tom Sawyer of our group. Remember when Tom got his friends to help him paint the fence? The same type of scheme was meted out by Royce. Example: if he wanted us to help with hauling hay, he would get us all pepped up about how much fun it would be and how afterwards we could all go swimming. To deny Royce was not an option.

While in high school, Royce won track events in the 100 yd. dash, 220 yd. dash, 440 yd. dash, 440 relay, mile relay, low and high hurdles, high jump, and broad jump. During his senior year, Vick Lewis, a former Aggie, and teacher at HCJC, took an interest in Royce and took him to several big track events where he participated against the largest schools. At the time Malakoff was a B class school, with less than 125 students in high school. I believe the largest schools were classified as 4A and the enrollment was much more than 125 for sure. He competed well with the bigger schools. One of the scheduled events he entered was in Dallas. Vick Lewis became his sponsor and took him to the big track meet. Later that summer, Royce was offered a scholarship to play football for Texas A&M and coach Bear Bryant. This was during the 1956-1957 season, the year after the infamous Junction summer. Many of the survivors of said torture camp were Royce's upper-class teammates. Royce was an active member of the Aggie Freshman team but unfortunately broke his hand when he stuck it into a facemask. This greatly curtailed Royce's Aggie participation and actually contributed to the end of his Aggie career.

My Early Football

It was not uncommon for Eddie and me to pass the football to each other in our front yards. We might spend hours just playing toss and catch, or sometimes we would play kick the ball. Of course, Eddie could always kick higher and farther than I, but we had lots of fun. One summer Mrs. Reese, a neighbor two doors north of the Nokes, had a visit from her daughter and Grandson, Kip. I was about 11 or 12 and Eddie the same, and Kip was maybe 8. It wasn't long before Kip came down to join us when we played football. Kip was almost as big as Eddie and certainly a lot bigger than I. This became a starting point of my learning to tackle. Eddie delighted in matching me up with Kip and watching me try to tackle him. He outweighed me by at least 30 or 40 lbs., but I somehow managed to bring him down even though he would drag me like a rag doll for several yards after I wrapped my arms around him. Eddie in the meantime, stood back and laughed. I am fairly certain Kip visited more than one summer and for more than one summer, thanks to Eddie, I was matched with this oversized boy in a man's body, of course to the delight of Eddie. Well, I suppose this is where my tenacity began or maybe I should say complete madness on my part, the hurling my little skinny body into that giant (and he was compared to me). The real test for my frail body came in Dodson's pasture, which was located on the East side of the highway, south of the Dodson's house and about a quarter of a mile north of the Sheltons. It is here the Dodson's sewer ran across the field and an abundance of grass burs were readily available. This is where the original Southside gang gathered to play games of football or baseball. It was tackle football with no pads and barefoot. Yes, we were barefoot, everyone went barefoot back then. Our feet were toughened from not wearing shoes during the summer. When we first moved into our house on Crossroads Drive, the road was not paved and either had sand or mud, depending on the weather. During the summer months, no question; it would have been dry, dry. When I crossed the road heading to visit the Dodson's, it was a given.... you had to "hot foot it" to cross the road. Once at the Dodson's the game was on. In the early days, Sallye and Thesea played with us, and it was a sad day for me when they stopped. Years later I understood why. Gathered on that field to play football, baseball, softball, or basketball included most of the neighborhood. In addition to Thesea, her brothers Royce and Sammy would be playing. Joining Sallye were her brothers, Rooster, and Tom Billy. Sometimes the Dodson's Grandson, Kenneth Willingham would enter the game. If you guessed I was one of the smallest, you would have guessed right. Tackling Royce, Eddie, Kenneth, or Tom Billy was nearly impossible for me, but I tried. On the way to Grandpa Roberts' place, along what is now Star Harbor Rd., there was the St. Paul Industrial School sign which read, "A quitter never wins and a winner never quits!" These words always echoed in my head. Perhaps what should have been echoing, "Don, what were you thinking?" When push came to shove, none of the players ever tried to take advantage of me, in fact they usually tried to go easy on me. The one-time Kenneth Willingham tried to bully me; Royce stepped in. Royce always stood up for the underdog, which I certainly was. It is with this background that I gained Royce's respect and later his urging me to go out for the Malakoff high school football team.

During the summer of '54, just prior to the start of football season, I had made my regular visit to the Gulf Coast and Jefferson County, visiting my Mother, Sister, and Stepfather. This visit as always resulted in several beach trips, thus allowing me to lose my pallor and gain a few pounds. During the summer months ever since I was 8 years old, I was separated from the Southside members for much of this time. Of course, Royce's exploits went on without me because he found others willing to follow, including Eddie. This particular summer I had actually grown a little and had a little more confidence. Maybe it was all due to the normal maturation process when my late blooming secondary sex characteristics began kicking in. As a sophomore at Malakoff High School, I decided to leave the band and join the football team, not as a player, but as the trainer. Coach Bishop was my freshman P.E. teacher/history teacher and he and I got along well. Royce told coach I would make a good football trainer and so I became the "gopher" for the team. I never realized how much work it took, helping to get equipment ready, taking care of the water, going back to the locker room to get things that were needed. I think I made the 1st game as manager and then I began to think, "Ok, playing can't be any harder than being manager and it would garner a lot more respect." After much pondering of the situation, I seriously thought about becoming one of the actual team members. My good friend Eddie was to be a starter as a sophomore and Royce would be starting as, a junior. There were other Southside members who were destined to be future starters. P.D., was in the 8th grade as well as Toothpick (Billy Joe) Robertson and Donnie Robertson were the other Southside members not yet in high school. Adding to that list were Rooster and Sammy, only 6th graders. Yours truly in today's jargon would have been labelled as a Nerd. By this time, I began to be self-conscious due to the start of pimples and acne. I desperately wanted and needed to be part of the team. The seniors on that team consisted of: Big and Lit Allen, Robert Lee Brannon, and Bill Smith; Juniors: Dickie Derden, Wayne Brown, Howard Hardy, Royce Shelton, Sophomores: Eddie Nokes, Ken Andrews, Harold (Bo) Johnson, Sonny Humphries, Freshmen: Hoss Cope, Ken Carroll, Joel Rogers, Gary Spivey, Tubby Washam, and Tony Womack. The more I stood and watched, the more I wanted to be in the midst of the action, not just a partial bit part as an unappreciated trainer. After several talks with Royce, he urged me again to go out for the team. I said, "They'll laugh at me." And he replied, "Not after the first day." So, I asked coach Bishop if I could join the team and he issued me a uniform. Because I had never played with pads, I knew nothing about how to put on a uniform. The first day, after I had finally figured out how to put on everything, I ran on to the field greeted by expected laughter. My helmet was a too large and the chin strap did not fit right. I felt rather clumsy in a full uniform. Immediately after my grand entry, Coach Bishop told me to line up on the right side as a defensive player. Malakoff's number of players was so small at the time; the only way to scrimmage was to have one side of the line offense and the other side defense. The very first thing I remember that day was my welcome to the team by Wayne (Johnny Mack) Brown. Wayne was playing tackle on the left offensive side (there was no right) and I was a defender on the right.

Wayne walloped me on my shin with his # 12, just as a reminder that I was a mere sophomore and welcome to the team. Mere love licks that hurt like the dickens, but I would not let anyone know for the world. The next thing I remember was a tackle I made. Hulan (Big) and Eulan (Lit) Allen (more nick names) were twins and starters. (Never understood the names because Big was actually the smaller of the two) Big was the fullback and Lit played on the line, but on occasion Coach Bishop allowed Lit to run the ball. This day, Lit ran the ball and right at me. In the past in Dodson's field, I had come face to face with tackling both Royce and Eddie, so I knew the only way to do was to grab the midsection, slide down and lock the ankles with my arms, so this is what I did with Lit. After dragging me for a few yards, he fell like a big oak. Embarrassed that a squirt like me did not bend when he ran over me, he told coach to give it to him again. Again, he was given the ball and blasted into to the line taking dead aim at me. Again, I repeated the same technique and down he went. Royce was right!! They didn't laugh at me after the first day and I became part of the team. My Grandmother did not know I was on the team until I brought my dirty uniform home for cleaning. After all of those years, I have wondered about that. When I was coaching Soccer at Spring high school, every athlete needed a physical and a signed parent permission slip. I suppose that was not required back then. I am not sure how I was able to convince my Grandmother to let me play, but nevertheless, I did. With the numbers as they were, I think Coach Bishop wasn't about to cut anyone as long as they were a warm body who might could be used as a battering ram and I definitely fit that description. There are a few other incidents I remember during my first year on the team. Robert Lee Brannon was our quarterback and one game he got his bell rung. A later description by the other players on the field gave me the rest of the story. Apparently, Robert was hit in the head and with today's rules he would have gone to the sideline and begun concussion testing. Back then it was holding up 2 or 3 fingers and asking, "How many do you see? "If the answer was wrong, then you went out of the game. There were times when the answer was given as three when there were actually only two. The reply was, "That's close enough!" I suppose he passed the initial tests because he remained on the field As they lined up in the huddle, he couldn't remember which play to call, so someone suggested one, which he replied that he didn't know that one. Immediately they called to Coach Bishop to get a replacement.

Another memory is when we played Eustace in Eustace and it was Cold!! I know the temperature had to be in the 30's and it was even colder sitting on Eustace's rock benches. The word "Bench-Warmer" was certainly a misnomer because it wasn't. So, I sat on that cold bench freezing to death, hoping for a chance to play. This was the last game of the season and I had yet to see a down of game play. After the score was well in our favor, Coach put me in at half back. I was so nervous that I forgot about the cold. I received the hand off perhaps three or four times and each time I felt as if I were blind and running in quicksand. Even the unskilled players of Eustace easily tackled me. As soon as anyone touched me, I went down quickly. At least I got to play a couple of downs!! Earlier in the season, prior to the Dawson game, while the Southside gang was playing football in Eddie's front yard, Royce ran slap-dab into the water faucet, which rose about two feet above the ground. I can't remember if it was his foot, ankle or both but whichever, he was limping. We were expected to run all over Dawson in our next game. Dawson, like us, was a small B class school and everyone knew that we were going to kill them. This was before Royce came up with his injury and even worse for me, I was slated as a potential backup. So, during the week, I tried my best to learn all of the plays which Royce would have been a part of. Reflecting on it, I don't believe Coach Bishop was ever serious about starting me in Royce's place, but none the less, I was more than a little nervous at the possibility. Royce did start (thank the Lord) and because of his limited playing ability, Dawson played us a really good game, but in the end we were victorious. From someone watching from outside, they would have thought Dawson had done an outstanding job of stopping Royce. Our team knew the real reason. I will always believe this contributed to what soon transpired, which I will explain later. After our season of '54 ended, there was an eager anticipation for the possibilities of an excellent '55 season. The core players were the same ones Neal Lawson (elementary principal and coach) had been working with since elementary school, and because this group had been together for several years it was thought they had a great chance of winning district and even beyond. During the summer of '55, Coach Bishop called for a meeting of our team at his house. I wish I could remember what was said, but I did come away with the idea this '55 year was going to be special. Later that summer, the bomb shell suddenly hit. Coach Bishop had been fired!! Why? It was rumored because he used cuss words to address players when chewing them out. This I never experienced. If I did, I don't remember it. Even if it was true, we all loved Coach Bishop. So, almost overnight, a bright new season with lots of great possibilities, suddenly was thrown into disarray. The new coach was going to be the same coach given credit for almost pulling off the upset against us. Yes, the Dawson coach, Bill Loggins. To this day I will always believe the powers that be thought Coach Loggins had devised a plan to stop Royce and the Tigers and it was with this false credit, coach Loggins was hired. In time we learned to love Coach Loggins, but it took a while. After the new season began, I remember Coach Bishop being on the sidelines as a spectator. It was apparent that he was very upset with the way he was treated and was carousing on the sidelines and talking to his former players. In those days, some of the attendees often walked the sidelines with the chain crew and moved up and down the sidelines with the ball. Coach Bishop was asked to leave and was eventually escorted off the field, while we all sadly looked on. There was nothing we could do, and though we felt for Coach Bishop we had a new season and a new coach. It must have been difficult for both Coach Loggins and Coach Farmer to experience this. I remember the seniors were not happy campers with what had happened and the early days of the season there was always a lingering chance of rebellion, but the senior leadership rose to the occasion and reacted in a mature manner. It was a really sad day when we lost to Ferris, 14-12 and after the game there was not a dry eye on the team. Due to the great senior leadership by Royce, Donald, and the other seniors, the Malakoff Tiger team finished the season without another loss. Mabank, our old rival, was the last game of the season and it was an away game. Mabank was really up for us and were predicted to give us a good battle. This November 18th game was cold, perhaps in the 30's. The Mabank Coach had told Coach Loggins what uniforms they would be wearing, but when we arrived, we found the uniforms they were wearing were not what they said they were going to wear. Our uniforms conflicted with theirs and so here we were set to play, and play could not begin. The solution: Dr. Haynes would drive a few of us back to our locker room, collect up the uniforms and then race back so the team could change into the new jerseys. It is with a very dim recollection that I tell you what happened. I do remember I was chosen to go back and help gather the correct color jerseys. Dr. Haynes probably broke laws as he sped back to Malakoff where the jerseys were gathered and then sped back to Mabank. All this time our team set on the bus trying to stay warm and almost didn't need any heat because the entire team was fuming. The Mabank strategy had resoundingly backfired because the longer our team waited, the madder they got. The result was an emphatic 49-0 shellacking. So, The Tigers finished the season a respectable 7-3 and second in district due to the 12-14 loss to Ferris. By today's standard we would have made playoffs. After most games meals were served to us at the Tiger Inn which consisted of really good chicken fried steaks, mashed potatoes, and white gravy. The meals always tasted better after a win but Mrs. Ruby McClain and my step grandmother, Mamie Rogers, knew how to cook those chicken fried steaks, so win or lose they tasted great!

My Football Injuries and other stories

I remember this as if it were yesterday. One of the practices that Coach Loggins had us do was one vs. one tackling and because of my sharp bones, no one wanted to pair up with me. As two people lined up it was decided which was the tackler, and which the runner. This then would be alternated. The tackler would run legs bent and place his shoulder squarely in the midsection of the runner, then hoist the runner up on his shoulder and carry him for several feet, driving the runner to the ground. This day, Joel Rogers, being a lower classmate, became an unsolicited volunteer to be my tackling partner. I think I was supposed to be the runner and Joel the tackler, but one or the other got mixed up and first thing I knew I was bleeding like a stuck pig when his helmet hit me squarely above my left eye. Perhaps that was because I did not wear my helmet for the exercise, which resulted in several stitches just above my left eye and having to sit out the next game.

Back in those days, we wore screw on cleats in our shoes and if you were stepped on it smarted. One day during workout, Marion "Tubby" Washam, stepped on my left hand, nailing me with his cleats. One of his cleats had come off, so instead of a cleat that nailed me, it was a screw. The resulting injury required Dr. Haynes to make an incision, sew up the wound and give me a tetanus shot. With hand bandaged I was not 100% for a while.

During two-a-days, morning, and evening football practice, I developed an injury to my back and could not lift my right leg more than a few inches. Of course, I could not practice, I went home thinking I would not be able to play in the afternoon. Mary Jo Norville was staying with us at the time, and she told me she could help my back, but I was skeptical. She had me lay face down on the bed and began massaging and manipulating, resulting in my full recovery and I was able to practice that afternoon. From this experience I learned Chiropractic and massaging works.

During one practice I was playing defense on the right side and the offense was practicing punts. I raced through the line, avoided the block, and jumped to block the punt, catching the ball directly in my midsection. All of the breath was violently knocked out of me, and I lay there gasping for air. I had blocked the punt, but now I was suffering for it. Coach ran over to see if I was OK and I remember asking him, "Did anyone get license of that truck?" In a few minutes I was back at it, none for the worse. The good Lord and his angels took care of my little skinny body, for which I am forever grateful. The only injury suffered during a game was our last game of the '56 season when someone blocked my left knee, knocking me down. I did get up and make the tackle, but my knee was slightly strained, and it was sore for a while, but with no future adverse effects.

When I was a junior, we were engaged in a scrimmage and when coach Loggins blew his whistle, the play was supposed to stop. Sonny Humphries, who was about my size, was known for his tenacity and his "never quit" attitude. On this particular play, Sonny had been knocked down by several players, but kept getting up, determined to tackle Donald Jordan. Donald had been given the ball, the whistle had blown, play had stopped and all of a sudden, Sonny tackled Donald. Donald outweighed Sonny by at least 50 pounds or better and after this untimely hit, Donald was fuming. The tackle had come from behind and long after play had stopped. He was ready to rip Sonny's head off. We all knew Sonny did not mean to hurt Donald; he was just a bit overzealous.

Buster Carter was known for engaging in "mouthing off" which he only did when there was plenty of distance between him and his target. On this day we were doing pass drills and Buster's P.E. class was on the field at the same time. Every time I ran out for a pass, Buster would who-rah me. "You can't catch a pass!!" About the third time, I had enough. The next time I ran out for the ball, instead of catching it and jogging back in, I took dead aim at my target who was spouting out verbal abuse to me. I ran toward him, knocking him down, and then stomped on him with my cleats. Buster and I were about the same size, and he always would "who-rah" people who were much larger than he because he knew they would not retaliate. The other reason, if there was some distance separating him from them. Coach screamed out at me, "Henderson, what are you doing?" "Nothing, Coach, I replied." And there were no more cat calls from Buster.

When we were preparing to go on our Senior trip, Eddie and I had told Sonny to tell Buster he was going to drown him if he went on the trip.

Sonny thought we were serious. Buster had suddenly decided not to go on the trip and the reason: Sonny had told him he was going to drown him if he went on the trip. We had to have a serious talk with Sonny because we were only playing around. Sonny was as serious as a heart attack, and it took some convincing to alter Sonny's mind. When we swam while in San Marcos for some reason Buster stayed on the banks.

Nicknames

We all had them, mine was Pedro. This was affectionately given to me by Tony Womack. One of the stories being read at the time was about a parrot named Pedro who squawked all the time and Tony said that fit me, so Pedro became my name. More people knew me as Pedro than my real name. Tony was the nickname giver, but I don't believe he had one of his own, and neither did Royce. Donald Jordan was "Belly," although I never knew why. "Sonny" Humphries was actually Clyde Corbin, but no one called him that. Marion Washam was "Tubby" and maybe he was as a kid. Billy Joe Robertson was "Toothpick" because he was anything but, just as "Fat man" was "skinny" Earl Ray Andrews. Billy Joe Magee became "Black Dog" after dying his hair black. Kenneth Carrol was known as "Cat" Carrol for some unknown reason. Ben Garcia's nickname came from the Disney Movie "Treasure Island" and the old hermit named Ben Gun. Once again, Tony Womack, after seeing the movie, chose Ben's nickname and it stuck. Paul Davis Bankston was P.D. which is obvious and because of Stanley Johnson's red hair he forever became "Red." Usually, the names all had some origin, though some origins were lost over the years. Albert Drake was a longtime bachelor who ran a gas station/grocery store and likely, Tony Womack picked the name "Miser Drake," which probably was an apt description considering the frugal life he led. Some even had multiple names. Because of my interest in science, I was known as "The Mad Scientist." "Home of the Mad Scientist" was even painted above my football locker. "Bones" or "Needles" was soon added to my entourage of nicknames due to my skinny elbows. "Sonny" Humphries was given the name "Fingers" when as a naïve Elementary student he let someone talk him into giving the middle finger to a teacher. We all later knew he didn't know what it meant. Earl Ray's other name was also Flacoocha for whatever reason. "Bo" Johnson was really Harold, but no one called him that. On occasion he was called "Hickernut" due to the shape of the back of his head. Eddie Nokes garnered the most nicknames and responded to all. I will try to name as many as I can remember. Eddie was known as: Lumberjack (his size), Pete (after his Grandfather, Pete Nokes), Burr Rabbit (his haircut), Tarzan (because of our Southside Tarzan call), and perhaps some more that I can't think of. Even teachers were not immune from nicknames as evidence by the name "Shemp" affectionately given to Mr. Pierce, named because he parted his hair in the middle and looked like one of the three stooges. Our principal, H.G. Larkin was affectionately known as "Hog Gut" (see initials). Naturally, the faculty nick names were strictly in house. Buster Carter could be added to the list, but I'm not sure if "Buster" was his real name or a nickname, because I never knew him by anything else. All of these names were given in fun with no malicious intent, and most names became part of a person's legacy. I suppose girls had nicknames, but I only knew of a few. Eddie Nokes little sister was Delores, but everyone knew her as Lokie.

Stepping Down From the Train

One of my earliest memories comes from downtown Malakoff. I was about 5 years old. This would place the time in the early 40's. My Grandmother and I traveled on a train from somewhere west of Malakoff. We likely boarded in Olney, Texas, which was the biggest town close to where we were living. I'm fairly certain that it was near Christmas time, and we were coming to visit my Great Grandfather and Grandmother, Andrew and Martha Roberts. Immediately after stepping off the train, I saw my cousin, Gary Jackson, standing at the front of Uncle Elmer's store. Gary was popping fireworks; evidence that it was near Christmas. Uncle Elmer's store was at the corner of the street that ran north/south on the southeast side of Malakoff's downtown, near the railroad tracks. The depot was just South of Uncle Elmer's store, as well as a small brick hotel on the south side of the tracks. In those days, the only time we had apples was at Christmas time and I can still remember the smell of those apples in Uncle Elmer's store. He sold them for 10 cents each and they were individually wrapped with a special paper. No other smell was like this unless it was Christmas morning when Santa came. When we walked into his store, I immediately smelled those apples and thought of Santa. How was Santa going to find me in Malakoff, way out in the country at Grandpa Roberts'? My Grandmother assured me that he would find me, but I was still very concerned. Looking back, I suspicion that this is where Santa found his apples to use Christmas Eve night, which must have been coming soon. Uncle Elmer's store seemed huge to me. He had glassed in cabinets with curved glass, so that he could display certain tempting ware for small boys. I was always drawn to those little cylindrical boxes containing peanuts with the promise of prizes of nickels, dimes or even quarters inside. I suppose this was one of the earliest forms of gambling for me. For a nickel you could get a box of peanuts and a chance to win me a big prize!! Back then a nickel was a nickel and would buy some good treats. Peanut patties and other candies also were there as a temptation. The other thing I remember from Uncle Elmer's store was his potbellied stove, stoked with wood and stood toward the middle of the store. It was cold this day and it felt good to back up to this warm stove. My Grandmother (Uncle Elmer's sister) spied what she was interested in. Uncle Elmer always kept a round wooden box on top of his counter. Underneath was "rat cheese" as my Grandmother described it. For a dime Uncle Elmer would slice off you a big piece of cheese and supply you with some crackers to satisfy your hunger. Grandmother loved "rat cheese" and so did I. The store was lined with shelves containing canned goods and toward the middle-right; there were bolts of cloth, which could be unrolled and cut for the women to make dresses. In the back of the store was the feed store part, which had a loading and unloading dock on the south side of the building. Outside, along that same east/west street was the Harrell Hotel (owned by Maude Harrell) a dwarf as described by my Grandmother. In the front, where Gary was popping firecrackers, is where Uncle Elmer kept his sack of feed on display. This old store had everything from groceries to livestock feed and was appropriately called a "General Merchandise Store". Downtown Malakoff was very active this day. Across the street I saw people going and coming from the Post Office, I remember seeing at least 2 drugstores, one on each side of the street. Cars lined the street and were parked at an angle. Back, farther north, on the west side of the street was Kirby's Grocery and Dry goods. My Grandmother walked me down to this store where we found it crowded with shoppers. I saw apples and oranges and nuts and other goodies that I hoped Santa would bring, but I was missing that concentrated smell of those apples as provided by my Uncle's store, which I can still smell today!! By the way, Santa did find me that night!!

Remembering Christmas Neighbors

This morning (December 2016) as I stood on my front porch in Spring, Texas, and my mind drifted back to the old days when I stood on my front porch in Malakoff, Texas. I saw in my mind as I looked to my left, Robert Nokes' Brickyard Truck. I knew inside my best friend Eddie would be up before long, popping firecrackers. On this Christmas Eve, so long ago, I could feel the anticipation in our neighborhood for tonight, when we all would gather around our individual trees to exchange gifts. Patsy and Lokie and Mrs. Nokes were inside and would be stirring soon. Mr. Nokes maybe had to deliver some bricks early today, while Mrs. Nokes likely would be working at Kirby Dry Goods at least part of the day. Diagonally across the street lived the Allens. This is where my good friend Henry lived, along with his older brother Wylie and their little brother Jimmy. Soon I would be hearing some good ole country hillbilly music oozing from their home, traversing all the way to us. It would either be coming from their radio or maybe Henry and Wylie would be singing and playing their guitars. Directly across the street lived Miss Willie West. It mattered not the temperature outside, Miss Willie, would have all her doors and windows shut tight. Later in the day there might be sounds of a piano playing. Miss Willie was a piano teacher and she often had students practicing. Perhaps on this day, some would be practicing for a Christmas recital. As I looked to my right, I saw a manicured hedge that separated our yard from the Day's yard. In front of the hedge in our yard was a Mimosa tree that would have lost its blooms by now and perhaps its leaves. Bill Day kept their yard immaculate, and he might be mowing today. Manny Day, the Day's youngest was a star Malakoff high school football player and starred later at East Texas State College. If he was home, he would be trying to get me to catch football passes which he enjoyed throwing as hard as he could. Somewhere inside were Charlie and Mable Day. Mrs. Day was the sister to Miss Willie, but they were not alike. I was told Miss Willie West was afraid to touch doorknobs and was always washing her hands indicating she had a germ phobia. One Christmas my Grandmother sent me to borrow a cup of baking powder from Mrs. Day for my Grandmother's cooking project. It wasn't until after the cake was cooked, we soon realized something went wrong. Did I really ask Mrs. Day for a cup of "baking soda" instead of a cup of "baking powder"? Diagonally and to my right was the Dodson house and inside that big house was my friend and classmate, Sallye, and her youngest brother Rooster, both still asleep in there somewhere. His name was Gordon Lynne, but no one called him that because Rooster seemed appropriate with his reddish colored hair. Pearl was likely in there cooking for their Christmas dinner and Dewey was hiding. The Dodson's often had big crowds of kin on Christmas Day and Pearl was the main preparer. Maybe Peal was working (she was once the telephone operator and also, she worked at Bankston's Dairy Queen) and might soon be driving by in the "Bat-Mobile" which is what we called their old maroon Oldsmobile. As soon as it was light, Tom Billy might have been out shooting baskets in their side yard, which was a magnet for us kids, even on days when it was cold. I am sure Rooster would have been out shooting fireworks before long and setting off chasers which would whistle down our street and then explode. South of the Dodson's up on the hill lived the Shelton's. For I.V. it was probably just another workday in the fields or perhaps a trip to Dallas to pick up a car to sell. Royce would have been up early feeding the stock or going to the Bradshaw's to milk the cows. Sammie would soon be going to play with Rooster because they were best friends. Several days earlier, my Granddad and I would have gone on our annual search for the right "Christmas Tree." Our search would have been east of our house in Robertson's field, near Walnut Creek. Granddad would have taken his saw with us and when he found an appropriate tree, he would have cut it down and toted it back home for decoration. Decorating the tree was an annual ritual, in which my Grandmother and I would engage. The tree would be secured in a metal holder or perhaps a rectangular plank attached to the bottom so it would stand straight. Sometimes we used popcorn, strung together in a long string, and wrapped around the tree from top to bottom. Fake icicles were strewn throughout the tree and finally a string of lights, of which there was always one bad light, making the entire string fail to light. The chore would then be to find the dead bulb by removing each bulb one at a time and replacing it until the bad bulb was found. At the top of the tree a star or an angel was placed. Cotton would surround and cover the bottom stand. After all of this was done, we could start placing our Christmas packages under the tree for Christmas Eve. It was not until years later when I learned about that type of tree we cut down. There it was several days before Christmas, where it stood in our living room. Little did we know, we were all allergic to Cedar. No wonder we thought we had a head cold!! It was tradition in our family to open our presents on Christmas Eve, as did everyone in our neighborhood. The Farrells, including Aunt Martha, Uncle Frank and my cousins John, Sam, and

Trina, would likely be there that night for our annual Christmas tree tradition. In my younger years I highly anticipated the coming day because during the night, Santa would be arriving with special gifts, as well as nuts, fruit, and candy. Of course, after learning the "secret" one must keep up the game; otherwise, Santa might not come. On Christmas Eve night, we would gather around the tree to open our packages in a particular way. All of the presents were handed out and then the oldest, which was my Granddad, would begin opening his first; then the next oldest and etc., until finally the youngest got to open theirs, providing their impatience and exuberance had not forsaken them. Trina and Sam would have been the youngest and Aunt Martha may have overlooked them tearing into one of their packages. There were never any big or expensive gifts, but all were given with love. Mommie (My Grandmother Grace) liked to give things she handmade. On Christmas Eve there would always be that one gift you forgot to get or perhaps something forgotten for the Christmas Dinner. In such case, a trip to town was needed and unless the Farrells had arrived, Granddad or I would need to walk to town. Downtown Malakoff was located approximately $1\ ^1/_2$ miles North of our house and it was pretty much a daily routine to make this trip on foot, especially for Granddad. The trip would have led us to Kirby's, perhaps on the dry goods side, where Cornnie (perhaps a Nickname for Cornelius) Kirby was the proprietor or if we needed groceries, on Leroy Kirby's side. Smith's Drug Store could well have been another destination, perhaps looking for that last minute gift. A visit downtown always led to a trip to my Uncle Elmer's store to say hello and wish him a Merry Christmas. Everyone would have been greeting each other with smiles and hearty hellos, all being in the Christmas spirit. The downtown area likely was full of angle parked cars doing their last-minute shopping. One annual occurrence for downtown Malakoff was the Smothers' St. Paul Industrial School visit with all of their orphans. It was the one day of the year when they came to town. I think they all must have been given a small amount to spend and were allowed to buy a few goodies. This was the one time of the year when the store had apples and that aroma floated throughout Kirby's grocery as a reminder Santa would surely bring a few to me the next day. Meanwhile, back at home, my Grandmother, owner of LaGrace Beauty Shop, may have had a few early customers before she began preparing for tomorrow's meal. Included in the meal was dressing, cranberry sauce, mincemeat pie, sweet potato pie, pecan pie, divinity, chocolate covered cheers (made days before if it was cold enough) Early Christmas morning the hen or turkey along with the dressing needed to be started. The drink of the day would be iced tea and in the early days we had no refrigerator, only an icebox, as did most of the neighbors. One of the things needed on Christmas Eve was a block of ice. If the iceman had not come, it was my duty to walk to the icehouse and bring home a small block of ice. It was carried with a string tied around it and by the time I arrived home the string would have cut its way into the ice. During cold weather it would not have mattered, but if it was warm day, a portion would have melted by the time I got home. The icehouse was located a short distance north of downtown and since it was the only place to get ice it was usually pretty busy, especially before a holiday. During the years when I still anticipated the arrival of Santa,

Christmas Eve would have been filled with eager thoughts of Santa coming. Even after the secret was out of the bag, Santa still continued to come. Not only would there be some special gifts, but also, candy, apples and nuts. Christmas Day would be filled with much fun; playing with the gifts Santa brought, popping firecrackers with Eddie, having a big Christmas dinner with the usual baked turkey or chicken with dressing, giblet gravy, cranberry sauce, and all sorts of desserts. My Granddad would read some scripture before the Christmas meal, relating to Christ's birth, followed by a prayer. I can still remember some of what Santa brought me. It wasn't until I "discovered" the secret that I realized; some of the things Santa brought actually were from my Mother who lived in Jefferson County at the time. Over the years, while in Malakoff, Santa brought things that I wanted. One year I received a microscope which was perfect for me because of my interest in science. Another time I received a Chemcraft chemistry set, and this launched my special interest in Chemistry and perhaps gave me a background for teaching. It was from this set that I earned my nickname of "The Mad Scientist" as I became the neighborhood Science Guy with demos of color changes, stinky concoctions, and explosions. I remember one Christmas; Eddie's Santa gift was a Gilbert chemistry set and this gave us both the ability to make stinky stuff and things that blew up. Eddie didn't progress with his chemistry set as I did, but he and I learned enough to hide under our desks when Bo Johnson and Kenneth Carter had the bright idea to collect hydrogen by dropping a piece of Sodium in a coke bottle and placing a balloon over the mouth of that bottle. It did produce hydrogen, but it also exploded and blew that coke bottle to smithereens. Eddie and

I both tried to warn them, but to no avail. Luckily, the only thing hurt was that coke bottle and perhaps some wet underwear (or worse) from Bo and Kenneth. From our chemistry sets, Eddie and I one day performed experiments on a several mice that we found. I can't remember exactly what we did do them, but they didn't live. Another Santa gift was my Red Ryder BB gun and I put it to use immediately doing target practice or shooting birds. The Red Ryder was a lever action made by Daisy. A few years later, Santa brought me a 50-shot pump daisy BB gun, with which I became an expert shot. One later Christmas Santa delivered a 22 single shot rifle to me, and this was when the era of BB guns quickly ended. Eddie, in the meantime, put away his BB gun and began using his shotgun. Whether Santa brought those guns, I'm not sure, but this is when Eddie and I began our team hunting with the rest of the core Southside Gang including Royce, P.D., and sometimes Rooster and Sammy.

CHRISTMAS FIREWORKS

During Christmas it was usually cold and popping fireworks was the fun thing of the day. The pain of one experience still lingers with me. We had some small firecrackers that were fun to pop and often they did not explode. It is a wonder I didn't lose a finger when I picked up that "so called dud" because it exploded in my fingers and boy did it hurt. My fingers were already cold from the outside temperature and when that firecracker went off, my already numb fingers from the cold were really hurting now. I remember crying, but I was too scared to go tell my grandmother and I recounted my fingers, making sure they were all there. During the firecracker shooting in cold weather, we would pop them for a while and then go in and warm up before going back out. Another game Royce dreamed up was to have firecracker fights. The idea was to light the firecracker and wait for it to burn down a little and then throw it at someone. The worst that happened to me was one exploding near my ears and being deaf for a while. This was not only stupid; but dangerous. Luckily, no one was ever really hurt, so once again the good Lord was looking out for us. Sometimes we had the TNT firecrackers, the ones with the fuse coming out of the middle and they were very powerful. We would place these under a tin can, light and run. The ensuing explosion would send the can high into the air. When we were younger, we had sparklers. When you lit a sparkler, it would burn and "sparkle." The fun part was whirling it in a circular motion so as to create a round light pattern. The other common thing was the Roman Candles. Roman Candles were in a tube about a foot or so long and after being lit, it would shoot out a flame, sending the fire into the air. There were several, maybe as many as 10 shots that could be fired. Sparkler and Roman Candles were shot at night and were great fun. The other thing we had were (N... Chasers). This politically incorrect term was used by everyone I knew, and I guess the only other name was just "Chasers". These would be lit on the road, or some smooth surface and they would take off and whistle going perhaps 20 or 30 yards and then explode. Eddie had cherry bombs, a round firecracker with lots of power. To add to the danger, Eddie chose to find a 10-foot pipe in which a ball bearing would just fit, and he used sawhorses to hold up the pipe. His target was 4ft x 4ft board about 10 feet away. He inserted the bearing into the pipe and placed the cherry bomb in the opposite end. He then lit the cherry bomb and quickly skedaddled, as I watched from a safe distance. When the Cherry bomb exploded that ball bearing shot out of the pipe and went completely through the board. Where it ended up, no one knows. Needless to say, **THIS WAS DANGEROUS**. I don't believe Eddie tried this again.

Recently I received a note from Eddie and what I just described wasn't nearly as dangerous as what Eddie said he made later. I am not even going to describe this project because someone might get hurt trying it. Another miracle of God that Eddie wasn't hurt.

Ice cream

The only ice cream we were able to get in the 40's and 50's was not the Bluebell variety that we know today. We were too poor to buy the store-bought kind in a large quantity, but we could buy a cone with one or two dips. We were not able to do this very often but on occasion we were able to splurge. A one dip cone sold for about 5-10 cents and a double dip for 10-15 cents. I recently bought a $1/2$ gallon of Bluebell, and it was over $6. Wow!! How times change!! That would have been close to a day's pay in the 40's and 50's. When we did buy ice cream from Kirby's grocery, it wasn't real ice cream, but was Mellorine, which was some diary product that resembled ice cream, but was full of air. If it melted there would be practically nothing left. We never owned one of those old hand crank ice cream freezers, but I did get invited to several ice cream parties in which homemade ice cream was made. This consisted of an apparatus which had a wooden barrel with a one-gallon metal container for holding the liquid ice cream recipe. After the ice cream mixture was poured into the metal container, the top containing the crank was put in place. Ice was placed around the container and then an ample supply of rock salt was placed on top of the ice. The crank was then put into place and an old quilt or blanket was placed on top. I quickly learned why I was invited. I was one of the persons "designated to crank." My job required a clockwise turning motion which was done until it became too difficult to turn. When this point was reached, the ice cream was done and ready to be eaten. What started out as a liquid of milk, eggs and sugar was now frozen ice cream which became our reward for cranking. The several kids and I who did the cranking were anxious to eat our masterpiece, but in those days, even though we did the work, the adults usually ate first. When the top was opened a whole gallon of ice cream was revealed and we ate until we were full enough to burst. This was indeed a special treat, especially on a hot day.

The only other time we were able to eat ice cream was if it snowed. My Grandmother would spot flakes of snow falling on a cold day and she would explain, "Mother Nature is plucking her geese!" As she said it, I looked, and it did look like feathers falling. Since we seldom got snow in our town of Malakoff, it was a thrill for a kid like me. As the snow began to cover the ground, my Grandmother said, "Ok, now we can make snow ice cream." This was music to my ears, because we did not get a chance to have ice cream very often. Never mind the outside temperature was cold, it would taste so... good. Snow ice cream was really like a snow cone with a mixture of eggs, milk and sugar poured over it, but for a 10-year-old poor country boy, it was delightful.

I remember it snowed a couple of times in the late '40's and perhaps again in the early '50's. When it snowed during the early '50's, Eddie and I decided to go rabbit hunting. We could view the snow as far as we could see. Looking across from mine and Eddie's house was a solid blanket of white, maybe at least a foot or more deep. What a thrill for two young boys, who loved to hunt rabbits. Dressed in our best "snow" outfits we were intent on tracking down a rabbit or two. The temperature was hovering around 30 degrees and even with boots on we were thinking our feet were going to get cold, but my Granddad had a suggestion to help. "Rub your feet with liniment," Granddad said. So, we did just that and I don't know if it worked but I know my feet felt hot. We both slogged through the snow looking for rabbits and never saw a one. We did have a snowball fight and some more snow ice cream along with a passel of memories.

Sugar Sack

Royce was always organizing some kind of game and "Chase" was one of them, only this time it was in Robertson's field east of our house. The entire Southside gang was gathered there, plus some honorary additions. One addition that I remember being there was Darla Robertson (now Allen) she and I were both in the Malakoff band. Darla was a lot taller than I, as was everyone else. Two honorary members that day were Stanley (Red) Johnson and Kay Kirby. The normal Southside Members were present, including myself, Eddie, Rooster, and Sammy. I don't believe P.D. was available for this activity. Royce was the decision maker as to who was on teams, and he set the rules. Over the years I have forgotten how I came to be without my pants, but there I was in my underwear, skinny legs, and all. I think the idea was if you got caught by the other team you got your pants removed if you were a guy. This rule did not apply to our only girl present. When Royce told me that he was going to take my underwear off, I took off, running like a scared rabbit. Reflecting on it, I know he could have easily caught me, as could anyone else, but I escaped to the back of the Allen's, where behind the house next to the Allen's was a trash pile which included a Sugar Sack. This Sugar Sack became my Sarong, which I was thankful to find. With this new wearing apparel, I made it home and was confronted by my Grandmother as to what happened and where were my clothes. After she heard my story, she immediately quickly walked to the Shelton's, madder than a wet hen. She confronted Dot (Royce's Mom) about what had happened and let her know in no uncertain terms that she was not happy with what Royce did; in other words, she told her "how the cow ate the cabbage". Dot's response ...she laughed about it, and this made my Grandmother even madder. I in the meantime was trying my best to get her not to go. My Grandmother was always "overprotective" but always on my side. What I didn't know until sometime later, Patsy and Lokie Nokes along with most of the neighborhood had seen me and my skinny naked body running across Robertson's field before I found that Sugar Sack. I think the entire time Royce was bluffing about taking off my underwear, but I believed him, and I was not taking any chances. As far as I can remember, nothing like this ever happened again. Another fine mess you got me in, Royce.

My Connections with Royce

In 1948 my Great Grandmother Roberts was very sick, and we moved back to Malakoff so that my Grandmother could help take care of her. Grandma and Grandpa Roberts and Uncle Bob lived out west of Malakoff on the north side of a dirt road, now a paved road named Star Harbor. To the west of Grandpa's house was a wagon trail that ran between Grandpa's 105 acres property and the next property. On the west side of that trail was a really small house and this is where we stayed when we first moved back. The Beets family (which included Randal Beets, a Malakoff school mate) later lived in this same house. I began going to the old Rock School in Malakoff in the 2nd grade. Across the street from Grandpa's and where we lived was the place once occupied by the Lucas family and later Dr. Kilman.

There stood a tin roofed house where the Shelton's lived; I.V., Dot, Royce, Sammy, and Thesea. This is where I first met Royce and the Sheltons. Royce was one grade ahead of me and Thesea one grade behind. Sammy had not started to school yet. We began walking to school together and this is where our friendship began. Our walk to the school was up that sandy road. There once was a cut through which traversed the Riddlespurger property and came out by the Old Malakoff Rock school. Along the way a sign was posted by the St. Paul Industrial School (A school for Orphaned Black children) operated by the Smothers family. It was a sign that I learned to live by. **"A quitter never wins and a winner never quits."** I can still remember cutting through the Vick Lewis's yard to get to the school. That walk with Royce to school was maybe as far as 2 miles. I don't remember the exact distance, but I do remember walking it. That road was very sandy unless it rained and then it was a muddy mess and difficult to cross. My family didn't have a car and I don't remember about the Sheltons, but nevertheless, we walked to school. Not too long after this we moved to our house on Crossroads Drive South of Malakoff. Sometime shortly thereafter, the Sheltons moved to their house about a quarter mile south of us. So, we were neighbors again. Many years would pass, and I had moved to Houston where my cousin John and I lived in Bellaire. Lo and behold, Royce moved to Houston and lived only a short distance from us. Several more years passed and after I married, my wife and I moved to Spring. Royce now lived a short distance away in the Woodlands area. So, over the years, Royce and I seemed to be destined to be near neighbors.

Sammy Shelton

Sammy Shelton was one of the Southside members and Royce's younger brother. Sammy and Rooster were two of our main members and often went with us on many of our excursions. It was Sammy who carried our dynamite, probably at the insistence of Royce. Sammy was quite different from Royce, both in physical appearance and personality. Sammy took more after his Mother, Dot, who had a lot of Indian blood. He had his mother's a dark complexion and dark hair. He was much shorter, and we knew from the beginning that he would never be the size of Royce. Like all brothers, he and Royce would often get into scraps, but in later years the scraps became more violent. To give you an idea of what I mean, one day while I was visiting the Shelton's, Sammy decided he had enough of Royce's teasing. I can't remember what that was all about, but what I do remember is the first thing I knew, Royce was ducking behind whatever he could find while Sammy was trying his best to plug him with a 22 rifle. I don't remember if he ran out of bullets or just decided to quit, but it ended without injury. I can still see, Royce dodging and running, hiding behind trees, or anything he could find. Royce was laughing, but not Sammy, He was intense and trying his best to shoot his brother. This was entirely out of the norm for Sammy, and it was quite scary. I was hesitant to stay around. This was enough to show me that Sammy had a temper and not as laid back as Royce.

There was a place called Tin Can Alley where we liked to gather, build a fire and camp out. It was a place where we could sit around the campfire and chew the fat, drink coffee, and relax. Tin Can Alley was located northeast of Downtown Malakoff and probably belonged to the Fuel Company. Over the years the place had become a dumping ground for cans and other litter, thus the name "Tin Can Alley" One night after building our fire and sitting around chewing the fat, we hear a loud "Wham!" a motor racing and then another "Wham!" This "Whamming" went on until we finally saw the source. It was Sammy driving his '57 Chevy. By this time Sammy was employed and had bought a used '57 Chevy from Danny Royal. Tin Can Alley was back in the woods and there was a narrow dirt trail leading to where we were camped. Sammy, being rather "juiced-up" (well actually he was Drunker than Cooter Brown) decided to join the rest of the Southside gang composed of Royce, Eddie, P.D. Rooster, and me. What we were hearing was Sammy failing to negotiate the trail without hitting trees and that "Wham" was occurring every time he hit a tree cluster. By the time he reached us, his car was battered, but it wasn't until the next day when he sobered up that he realized it. None of the rest of our gang was drinking, only Sammy. At the time we all thought it was funny, but looking back on it I have come to realize that it was not. The next day Sammy lamented "What happened to my car?"

In about 1965, my Aunt Martha and Uncle Frank Farrell set up a pool hall in downtown Malakoff called the Cross-Cues. John and Sam, my cousins (both occasional Southside members) helped to run the pool hall. John made a deal with a guy who was a gasoline distributor. He brought and set up a gas tank in my grandparent's front yard in exchange for unlimited pool shooting at the Cross Cues. John was staying with my grandparents at the time while he helped run the pool hall. Late one night there was a knock at the door and John awoke to find Sammy Shelton standing there with a gas can. "My car ran out of gas, and I need some. Could you please give me enough to get me to a gas station?" Of course, John gave him a little gas. John used his own car to carry Sammy back to his car which was at the foot of the Shelton's driveway where it sat after it had run out of gas. Sammy opened the hood on that '57 and as John stood looking on, Sammy began pouring gasoline all over the engine, while exclaiming, "This blankity blank car has run out of gas on me for the last time!!" and in one motion he threw a match on the engine. Immediately the whole engine went up in flames as John stood dumbfounded. John quickly exited the situation and returned home, later hearing a siren as the Malakoff Fire department responded to a car fire.

Rooster Dodson

I first met Gordon Lynne Dodson, better known as Rooster, shortly after we moved to our new house located south of Malakoff on the west side of the road to Crossroads. The meeting was more of an encounter than a meeting. It had just rained, and a ditch of water was in front of our house. This red-headed kid was walking along the edge of the ditch and the mud road. It wasn't until several years later that this road to Crossroads was asphalted and at the time it was a muddy mess due to the rain. I can still hear those original cusses coming out of Rooster's mouth, which went something like this, "Dod damn ton-ah-bitch!!" He repeated this same phrase several times and I to this day do not know what he was cussing about, but whatever it was he was doing it in a tongue-tied fashion. Over the years there would be many other meetings with my red headed friend and more cursing I am sure, but this is the one that sticks in my mind. Rooster was about four years younger than me, so I figure I was about 8 and he about 4 at the time. I soon learned that Rooster lived diagonally across the street in the big white house with the porch. His Mother was Pearl, and his Dad was Dewey. He lived there with an older brother Tom Billy and an older sister Sallye, who was in my same grade at school. The family consisted of several older brothers and sisters who would often visit. The Dodson house was always a beehive of activity, especially at special times like Thanksgiving, Christmas, and Easter. In their side yard was a field consisting of several acres and encompassed the area all the way South to the Shelton's place. This is the area where the Southside gang gathered in later years to play tackle football. We played barefoot and without any pads. The pasture had some sewer running through it, which we had to avoid, as well as sticker burs that often stuck in our feet. When Rooster was this age, he didn't play football with the rest of us, but his sister Sallye did. Sallye, having once competed with several older brothers, was just as tough as any of the guys. It was a sad day for me whenever she quit playing with us and it wasn't until years later that I realized why. Sallye had changed from a girl to a woman. The Dodson home became one of our central gathering places where we either played tackle football or shot hoops on their basketball goal. Often it became tackle basketball also. The court did not lend itself to dribbling, so it became a basketball running game. I was pure clumsiness at this early age and only Rooster and Sammy were smaller than I, but this is where I soon learned to be tough.

When Rooster was about 10 or 11, he was known to sleepwalk. One night, according to his sister, Sallye, he went to sleep under their big porch. It was a warm summer night and Rooster had played all day and was tired and sleepy. The Dodson's house had a front room and immediately behind it was a dining room. To the right of the front room was a bedroom. Behind the bedroom in later years was the location of their bathroom. A wraparound porch and a separate bedroom were found on the Southwest corner, not connected to the rest of the house. Under this section is where Rooster fell asleep. Located a short distance south lay the pasture where we played football. On the far south side of the pasture the Shelton's house stood. One night after Rooster had been sleeping under his house he must have sleep-walked across that pasture and went to Shelton's back door. He proceeded to knock on their back door at about 12 midnight. Dot, Royce's mother, came to the door and asked, "What in the world do you want at this time of the night?" Well,

Rooster mumbled something, and Mrs. Shelton soon came to realize that Rooster was not awake. Soon he awoke and exclaimed, "What am I doing here!!" to which Mrs. Shelton replied, "That's what we wondered!!" On several occasions later, Rooster did the same thing…he was sleep walking.

The bedroom, located to the right of Dodson's front room, was where Pearl would often entertain the ladies from her Church group. Everyone in our neighborhood had outdoor toilets at one time and theirs was located in the same pasture where we played football. It was several years later that the Dodsons joined the more elite and added an indoor toilet and bathtub, thus eliminating the use of the #3 tub as well as the trip out back when nature called. Kenneth Willingham (the Dodson's grandson) was visiting from Fort Worth and decided to have some fun one night when Rooster was bathing. There had been reports of a "window peeper/prowler" in the neighborhood and everyone was well aware of the person, and all were on alert. In those days, no one had air-conditioning, only small fans, so windows were left open (often without screens) to catch whatever breeze might be stirring. This particular night, the women from Church were gathered in Pearl's room, either just to meet and gossip or perhaps to do quilting, which they often did. Anyhow, all were gathered in the room next to the bathroom where Rooster was bathing. Kenneth reached his hand in the window from outside and dangled it over Rooster's head, never saying a word. When Rooster saw that hand, in his mind that was the prowler and he arose quickly out of that tub screaming and ran buck naked into the bedroom with all those Church women, slipped and fell on the floor screaming, naked as a jay bird. I happened to walk into the house for a casual visit, just as he hit that bedroom in his unclothed condition. At first the women were completely shocked to see an undressed man come flying out of that bathroom and then the screams scared the socks off them. Needless to say, this quickly broke up whatever meeting the ladies were having, and Pearl grabbed a large towel and wrapped around a naked dripping, very frightened kid. By this time Kenneth had come back inside and was dying with laughter. I soon realized that Rooster wasn't hurt, so I too had a good laugh. Naturally, Mrs. Dodson was indeed embarrassed, but as usual, she took it in stride. You need to remember, back then, everyone in the neighborhood often visited each other and we might give a light tap on the door and then give a holler and walk on in. This proved to be another surprise incident that happened to me. It was long before the Dodsons' had indoor facilities and still used that old faithful, the #3 tub for bathing. I was looking for Rooster one day and gave a holler and then proceeded to walk in the front door without knocking. Much to my surprise and also, Pearl's, I suddenly found Pearl taking a bath in their #3. Pearl was on the large size and though she quickly covered herself and screamed bloody murder, it was difficult in that little tub for her to hide. Meantime, I was so embarrassed that I quickly closed my eyes and left Dodson's in a hurry, "Sorry, Pearl." From that day on, I did not go in without someone letting me in.

One time near dusky dark, Rooster, Sammy, Eddie, and I decided to ride our bikes down the road south to the Negro cemetery, located approximately one mile from our houses. It was summertime and though it was getting dark, there was still enough light to clearly see. Eddie was usually the one in the lead because he was the strongest, followed by me, then Sammy and last, Rooster. As darkness began to set in, and we arrived at that Black folk's graveyard, all sorts of scary things begin to creep into our minds. Naturally, all of us pretended bravery, which was indeed fleeting. I remember my heart pounding as I thought about those ghosts that might be there. On our return trip, we all began peddling faster, but since it was a sandy road, progress was much slower than we would have liked. On our return trip, the same sequence of Eddie, then me, then Sammy, and in the rear Rooster. It really was scary to all of us, and so our adrenaline was pumping like crazy and so was our imagination. All of a sudden there was big loud "bang!", and this black thing came flying by. In our minds it was one of those buried black ghosts that had arisen and was after us. We all were pedaling as hard as we could and were making a rapid exit from that graveyard. Rooster as always was bringing up the rear, but all of a sudden, we heard him holler and he hurled his bike into the ditch and took to foot. On foot he passed us all. Rooster was the first back to his house by a good 50 yards or better. It wasn't until the next day that we were brave enough to go back to that cemetery, but only when it was broad daylight. Upon investigation we found the black ghost. What had happened, as Rooster trailed us, his bike had a blowout and somehow, that busted inner tube came flying forward, high in the air, and for four frightened white boys, we just knew it was a Negro cemetery ghost. How in the world Rooster passed the three of us on foot has remained a mystery all of these years, but I guess that adrenaline can do strange things, at least it did that time!!

DUMB BUM

The title, "Dumb Bum" will be explained in due time, but it all centers around our front yard and football play. My cousins, John and Sam Farrell, came to visit us often in the early 50's and when they did, a football game was certain to take place in our front yard. Rooster Dodson would come over to partner with John against Sam and I. Sam was about 5 or 6 years old and was small enough to just fit under my legs as he did his imitation of a Quarterback sneak. With Sam as quarterback, he would toss me the ball and I would catch and run against Rooster and John. Rooster was the QB for John most of the time. Everything went fine until Sam got hurt. Of course, we played tackle!! I was the oldest and the biggest (probably the only game I played back then when I was) and I took advantage of it. Usually, Sam and I won because that little bugger could toss the football pretty good. As I said, everything went fine until Sam got hurt and then he would yell, "Dumb Bum!!" which became his favorite by word when he was upset. When he yelled his by word, football was over and Sam would go and sit and cry, but 5 minutes later we would be back at it again, at least until Sam said the words DUMB BUM again. Years later, Sam was the quarterback for the Seymour junior high and high school team until he had a severe knee injury. During junior high he won numerous track events and was an over-all good athlete. Rooster Dodson was destined to be Malakoff's starting quarterback his Senior year and I would like to think I had a part in both their successes due to those early football games in our front yard so long ago.

ROOSTER, JOHN, AND SAM IN OUR FRONT YARD

This is the yard where we had our football games. In the background you can see the Nokes' house and yard, where all sorts of games were played.

Jeep, Jack Rabbits, and Juice

Paul Davis (P.D.) Bankston was the South Side member with the widest range of transportation. His Dad, Paul, owned the Olds Dealership and P.D. had the privilege of driving a new Olds. Eddie, Royce, and I often rode with him on trips to Athens after our yearnings turned from guns to girls. P.D. also had a WW II Jeep, in which the four South Side members often rode. Riding in the Jeep was a fun activity. We were in the open and could go pert-near anywhere, and we did. In order to accomplish this, we needed to go onto property that was posted. Cedar Creek was just a Creek then with no Lake; that came later. This was probably '54 or '55 when we made our excursions in that old jeep. It would traverse muddy embankments and even go through shallow water. We went up hills, down hills, through thickets, almost anywhere. P.D. was the owner and the driver, while Royce, Eddie and I clung to anything we could grab as P.D. raced over the terrain. During one excursion we ventured onto one of these Posted properties, where we ran into a problem. As we started to exit the gate where we had entered, we found it locked. P.D. found the only solution to get out of there and in a hurry. He blasted the lock with his shotgun.

One night we decided to go onto some posted property near Cedar Creek to hunt for Jack Rabbits. With shotguns in hand and tobacco juice in mouth, off we raced in the jeep, hoping to find a rabbit. In the 50's Jack Rabbits were fairly common, but they were too fast for us when we were on foot. Royce came up with the perfect solution: "P.D. what if we used your Jeep and chased down those Jacks with that!! It would be fun at night!" So, P.D. agreed and there we were, chasing Jack Rabbits in his Jeep that night, with P.D. driving and Eddie, Royce and I holding our shot guns, our jaws full of a tobacco chew. I think P.D. was the only one Not chewing tobacco that night, in fact I don't think he ever did, but Eddie, Royce and I had our mouths full of Beechnut juice. As we rode along, hoping to spot a Jack Rabbit, one jumped up. As we highlighted him with the headlights, guns ready to shoot, all of a sudden, we hit a big hole. Gravity took over and we first dropped about 3 or 4 feet and then bounced, landing Ker-plop on the other side of that hole. After P.D. finally was able to get stopped, we quickly examined ourselves to see if we had all our parts. Well, to our surprise, Eddie was no longer in the Jeep. P.D. had finally stopped at least 20 yards from that hole and at that bounce, Eddie had fallen out. There he sat, shotgun in hand, trying to decide whether to rub his head or his belly. Unable to decide which needed his attention the most, he sat rubbing both. When we hit that hole, we all bounced up, Eddie included. Only thing, Eddie, hit his head on one of the shotguns when he bounced up. As he did, he swallowed his chew and fell out. There he set in the field rubbing his head from hitting the gun and his belly from swallowing his chew. When we realized he was OK, of course we began laughing, but not Eddie, who by this time was turning green from his unintended swallow. This ended our Rabbit hunt for the night.

Hay Hauling

Every summer Royce would call upon Eddie and me for some fun in the sun. One of the only ways to make money around Malakoff was hauling Hay. The hay would already be cut into square bales, not like the big round ones you see today. Early in the morning Royce would either be knocking on our doors or giving the Tarzan call to alert us that something was about to take place. He might have even prepared us for it the day before, none the less, we were in for a day at the hay field. Royce was the designated tractor driver, and he would drive the tractor along a path as Eddie and I loaded and stacked the hay in rows on the trailer. Sometimes we had an extra hand like Sammy to help. It was hot work and the earlier we started the better. There was no such thing as cool when you are out in the East Texas sun in July and August. Loading was the cool part; the hot part came when we got to our destination, the barn loft. It was in this loft, if we were lucky, the temperature would only be around 120. As with everything else, Royce liked to make a game of it and see how fast we could load. He pushed for Eddie and me to load that hay as fast as we could. Since Eddie was stronger, he could load a lot faster than I. We each wore gloves and carried a hay hook with us which we used to grab the bale. Each bale was wrapped with baling wire or in some fields twine was used (the same twine that I remember from the icehouse). The initial step of the bale being placed upon the trailer entailed hooking the hay hook into the hay, grabbing the wire or twine with the other and hand and swinging the bale onto the trailer. I don't remember ever wearing a hat because Royce said, "Aw, you don't need a hat, Don, it's not that hot!!" When we arrived at the barn, Royce would back up the trailer so that one could stand in the trailer and lift the bales up to the other two in the hay loft. Royce was the one who lifted up to Eddie and me and then it was our job to grab with the hay hook and pull into the loft and stack nicely. Naturally Royce would make a game of it and challenger us to work faster. I always longed to have been born stronger so that I could have been the one in the trailer where it was a good 20 degrees cooler, but as genetics would have it and the pecking order already established long before, the loft was mine and Eddie's. From sunup to sundown we labored, often making several trips to the same barn and sometimes to several, all for about a penny per bale. That doesn't sound like much, but for us poor boys, it would buy plenty. Then there was the time we loaded up that trailer and stacked it as high as we could stack it. We then took off for the barn loft and even over the bumps it held fine until we encountered an overhanging limb. That limb knocked off a good portion of the stacking. All our earlier work, gone in an instant. Royce began laughing and set us immediately to work, taking as long to re-load as when we first loaded the hay. Did I mention that in the old days, we did not lift weights as training for football or any sport? Who needed it?

This is a poem written about our hay hauling and another of Royce's manufactured games. **Royce's Hay Games**

By Don Henderson 7/9/16

Hay Fields and Barn Lofts Hot, Hotter

Square Bales Smell of New Cut Grass

Sweat, Baling Wire Hay Hooks

Royce, Laughing, Making a game of

Hay-Hauling

Tobacco Chewing, Stain running down truck doors,

Truck loaded to the hilt Bouncing over Rough Roads

Losing that Load

Royce Urging.... COME ON!!

It's fun, This having to

Re-Load!! Tired!! Hot!!

Fun??

NOT!!

Re-Loaded,

Again on the way

With that load of hay

Off to that Barn

120 in the Shade

But, there's money to be made

Besides, It's fun!!

Watermelons

In the 50's the only time we were able to get watermelons was during the summer around July 4th. Close to that time we would anticipate Tom Davis driving his tractor and trailer by, loaded with watermelons. His watermelons were the dark green round ones about double the size of a basketball. He had another variety the shape somewhat like a football only bigger and longer. To obtain a good one it was necessary to thump the melon with your hand and listen for the proper sound. It was that hollow, ringing sound you looked for, indicating it was ripe. You could trust Mr. Davis to pick a good one if you so desired. We usually bought the 25-cent variety because it was smaller and just the right size for our family. Any more than a quarter would have been a lot for us to spend back then. You could buy a medium sized one for 50 cents and a huge one for 75 cents. The watermelon feast would come after we made our purchase. Our kitchen table would be spread with newspapers to catch the runoff juice or maybe we would eat it on the front porch. If it was the round type of watermelon, it would be cut in half and then the half would be sliced into smaller parts. It was always fun to use a teaspoon and channel out a piece by making a round motion. Before this, salt was liberally supplied. There was no such thing as a seedless melon back then. This was especially true of the Black Diamonds which had large seeds. These were spit out as you ate. A good watermelon was sweet and juicy and on a hot day like July 4th, it was refreshing. Since in the early days we had no refrigerator, we usually ate the melon as is. At Grandpa Roberts' place, he would put the melon into a bucket made for drawing up water and then lower it into the water well. After it was left there a while, the melon would then be fairly cool. We then would sit on his front porch and eat until we were full. Afterwards the left-over rinds would be thrown into the yard where the chickens would feast. Grandpa sometimes raised his own melons because his soil was sandy, perfect for watermelons.

The Southside Gang, led by Royce decided one day to visit a local watermelon farm and sample a few right off the vine. Royce suggested we go at noon because he figured it would be too hot for anyone else to be there. The best way to do this was to cut the watermelon open with a pocketknife and then reach into the middle or heart with your hand and collect a chunk to eat. This was done quickly right in the field, but then, "Hey, Royce, I hear someone coming!!" At that alert our meal quickly ended. My heart was racing, and we needed to get out of there fast. It became a race to the fence to get out of there. We had heard the farmer kept a shotgun loaded with rock salt for just such occasions. Royce scrambled over the top of that 3-strand fence like a graceful deer, while Eddie and I chose going through the middle-barbed wire. I hung the back of the shirt on a barb and had to frantically rip it loose. Eddie barely was able to get through as the farmer fired a warning shot into the air and my heartbeat even faster. The sweet watermelon taste had quickly been replaced with the bitter thought of rock salt blistering our behinds. Royce, as usual was laughing to beat sixty and Eddie and I were leaving that field like a couple of scared rabbits. This was the first and only time we ever tried to swipe a watermelon. Once again, Royce, another fine mess you got me into.

Chinaberry Fights

Growing up in Malakoff, Texas during the 40's, 50's and 60's included making up our own games. This was long before any of us knew anything about modern day paint guns. In my backyard grew a China Berry Tree. This is not the Chinese Tallow, which is a different variety all together. This tree was approximately 20 + feet tall and bloomed white flowers in the spring. The newly formed fruit became our ammunition to chunk. A crop of thumb-sized green berries resulted and there was always a plentiful supply. We would each gather a handful of berries and proceed to "chunk" them at our opponent. Sometimes we played cowboys and Indians and if there were as many as three of us, each was on his own. An established rule was set before the game began and if you got hit in a "kill-zone" you were out of the game. Most of the time we just kept throwing until we got tired, or someone started crying from being hit in the face. I often had China Berry fights with my cousin, John. Without fail I would accidentally cause him to begin crying. When I did, I was in trouble and my Grandmother would require me to retrieve my own switch, perhaps from that very tree. Then John and I would both be crying. The onslaught of China berries peppering you could indeed sting and hurt like the dickens. The wood of the tree itself, did not lend itself to climbing because the limbs were very brittle. On more than one occasion I tried it, only to fall when a limb broke. I remember landing on my back "Ker-Plop" and getting the breath knocked out of me. I ended my China berry tree climbs after that. I remember a story my Granddaddy told me about my Dad, Albert and his brother, Preston. They climbed to the top of a China

Berry tree when they were kids. My Dad bet Uncle Preston a dime that he could beat him down. Well, as they both scurried down as fast as they could, a limb broke and Uncle Preston fell, landing on his back knocking his wind out. My Dad reached in his pocket, gave Uncle Preston the dime, and said, "Here's a dime, you won fair and square!!" Back to the China Berry fights, they all would start out in fun but often ended up with one or the other mad. A red whelp on the face showed the scars of battle and maybe if a berry landed in the eye, it would really hurt for a while. I don't remember any girls ever playing this game with us, but I am sure we had some who were tough enough, especially Eddie Nokes' little sister, Lokie, or maybe our neighbor across the street, Sallye Dodson. The berry fights were all in my yard because I don't think anyone else had a chinaberry tree. Royce Shelton's sister, Thesea would have joined in, but we didn't ask girls to be in our game. This game was strictly a Spring/Summer/early Fall game because after the first cold spell, the green berries would begin to ripen into a mushy yellow-brown and not a good projectile. After the berries turned yellow, they would then begin to ferment, and I often saw mockingbirds eating those ripened berries and getting wobbly drunk. The berries are poison, though I never saw any terminally ill affects to birds. There was one kind of bird which Eddie and I called "BB" birds. When a flock landed in a tree and we shot one of them, the others wouldn't bother to fly. Once Eddie even killed one with a home-made blow gun (which is another story) Later we learned that the BB birds were Cedar Waxwings, and they love to eat ripe Chinaberries. The entire flock would be "wobbly". For this game, we didn't need any equipment other than what nature provided.

Corn Cob Fights

When it came to organizing a game, no one was better than Royce Shelton. Royce was good at everything, well pert near. I'll talk about that later. I suppose you could call Royce our commander-in-chief, whether it was for a game of some sort or a work project like hay hauling. To get to Royce's house it was a short trek from my house, down the hill south on the road to Crossroads about 200 yards and then turn left up the hill to his house. In the back of the Shelton's, they had a barn with a plentiful supply of our ammunition in the form of corn cobs. I.V., Royce's Dad raised corn in other locations and the corn was picked for the Shelton's livestock. If you know anything about a Corn Cob, you will remember that where each kernel attached, a depression naturally remained after the removal of a corn kernel. You have heard the expression "rough as a cob", well a Corn Cob is just that. This is useful to know if you are going to battle with Corn Cobs. The first step is to gather all the cobs you can find that are remnants from the animal's meals. In the meantime, you needed to avoid the numerous cow paddies that dotted the landscape. Most of the time, we carried our ammunition in a bucket or a tow sack. (In case you are wondering, a tow sack once housed feed for the livestock) Of course the Corn Cobs needed to be soaked in water to give them that nice soggy appearance with the capability of inflicted pain on your opponent. Royce, as the leader, would be the one who decided teams. Most of the time it was Eddie, me and Rooster and against Royce and Sammy or maybe Eddie and I would get Sammy and Royce Rooster. Royce would sometime choose me for his team member against Eddie, Rooster and Sammy. This was the team

I really liked!! Others sometime joining in the fray included Red (Stanley) Johnson, Kay Kirby, and Rooster's kin, Kenneth Willingham. When Eddie and I were in the 7th grade, Kenneth Willingham moved in with the Dodsons. Kenneth's Mother was a Dodson and though he had only visited before, for some reason he moved to Malakoff to live with his grandparents. I mention Kenneth because I remember at the time; he was a better athlete than Royce. He was faster and had more natural athletic ability than any of us. It wasn't until several years later that Royce became #1 as far as athletic ability and Kenneth lost ground because he began a downward spiral, which included cigarettes and alcohol. One of our team-cob members was James Surls who was about the same age as Rooster and Sammy. (James Surls today is a world-renowned artist). Perhaps he developed some of his artistic skills while dodging corn cobs, rubber bands or mud balls. Our battle ground was around the barn, where there were plenty of hiding places, if you could avoid the mud and previously described patties. You definitely wanted to avoid the "fresh" patties, or the Chicken poop that was scattered everywhere. Since we all went barefoot most of the time, cleaning just involved climbing into the watering trough and rinsing, but don't let I.V. catch you doing this. Wearing blue jeans was a distinct advantage because it did prevent getting a "Corn Cob Tattoo" on your legs! The rest of your body was open game. And by today's rules you even can't play dodge ball for fear someone might get hurt. If you have ever been hit by a wet Corn Cob, chunked by a bigger kid, like Eddie or Royce, you would know how it feels. Eddie, being creative, would get added distance with his cob by using two chicken feathers in the end and when he threw it, that sucker would sail. Rooster and Sammy could chunk pretty hard too, but not nearly as hard as Royce or Eddie. What you didn't want to do was get hit in the face. We had an un-written rule; we did not deliberately hit anyone in the face, though on occasion it did happen. A red whelp would immediately appear, but by the grace of God, no permanent damage. Our Corn Cob fights would last for as long as someone didn't get hit in the wrong place, we ran out of Cobs, or someone went home crying. Corn Cob fighting was a fairly routine event that usually happened when we were supposed to be doing some sort of work for Royce's Dad. Without fail, we all would rather play. Again, corn cob fighting was one of Royce's games. In addition to fighting with corn cobs, there were other things that I learned to do with them. At my Great Grandpa Roberts place because of all of the livestock he had, corn cobs were plentiful. By placing two feathers in the end of the corn cob you could throw it up and it would sail for a good distance. You could also make a good dart out of a corn cob by adding a pin or a sharpened nail to the front with feathers in the back. We could entertain ourselves for hours with all those free cobs. This activity at Grandpa Roberts place was with my cousin Gary Jackson, who was about 5 years older. Gary was somewhere near 10 and I probably about 5 or 6 when we played all over Grandpa's yard, either with corn cobs or chunking black walnuts from the huge tree in Grandpa's front yard. Gary talked me into going up into the barn loft and hurling a feathered corn cob to the ground. We both made good flights until we ran out of our supply of cobs. We were up, and after our toss, our reserve supply was on the ground. Gary challenged me to jump out of the loft to retrieve my sailed cob and stupidly I met the challenge, only to land with a thud, knocking the breath out of me. Believe you me, I never tried that again. Of course, Gary knew better and was smart enough not to jump. It was a wonder that I didn't break something. The Lord takes care of stupid kids. Thank you, Lord!!

Mud Ball Fights

Across from my house on the east side was Robertson's property where we often roamed. I remember the color of the soil around the small tank was red because of the iron content. The clay in the tank was likely the same type used by the brick yard (the brick yard was located to the west of my house). The word "tank" is a descriptive word used by Texans for a small pond. We used this "tank" in many different ways even though it was supposed to serve as a watering place for cattle. The tank was too shallow to swim in and besides all that, it was very dirty looking. Occasionally we would go craw-dad-in there. To crawdad we used a pork rind tied to a string and those red crawdads would latch onto that pork rind with their strong pincher, and you could catch a good-sized crawfish. I remember taking my prize home, all excited with my first catch. This excitement turned to pain, when that crawdad clamped down on one of my fingers!! I quickly learned that you better catch that bug from the backside away from those pinchers. Of course, Royce would never say a word when one pinched him, pretending that it didn't hurt a bit. I tried this, but it didn't work; I could only pretend for so long. When I got home with my "prize" I asked my Grandmother to cook it for me, but since the only thing with any meat on it was in the tail, the total meal was a small bite (maybe enough to fill a hollow tooth). This of course was long before today's version of boiled crawfish that many restaurants serve as a delicacy. Once while seining in the tank, we caught a really odd-looking critter. I was told it was a salamander. I later learned that it was mud puppy and years later I learned that this was the larval stage sometimes called a water dog. On the banks of this tank is where we set up our mud fights. We had a plentiful supply of ammunition because all we had to do was grab up a handful of that red mud and form it in our hands, then it was ready to hurl at the nearest opponent. Splat that mud ball would clobber your nearest mud ball opponent. By this time, you would have mud everywhere; mud from wadding, mud on your pants, on your shirt, in your hair all over. I have seldom been able to be in a snowball fight, but from what I can gather, a mud ball fight is very similar. Occasionally some devious individual would put a rock in the middle of the mud ball and if you got hit with one of those it would really hurt. The plain mud might sting, but the one with a rock would definitely hurt. If Royce got you with one of those or a regular one for that matter, he'd break into his laughter; but if he got hit, he pretended that it didn't hurt, so we would try and do likewise. I once got hit slap-dap in the face and I strongly suspicioned with a "Mud Ball alteration", in other words a rock in the middle. I screamed but dared not cry; for fear that our leader would think I was a sissy. Naturally I could not let my grandmother know what had happened because she would go flying down to Royce's home and confront Dot, Royce's Mom. My Grandmother was, in my mind, always overprotective and I didn't want her interfering, but after having my own kids, I now better understand. If Rooster got pelted really good, he would not hesitate to exit the battlefield in a hurry and head for home, maybe crying. Sammy on the other hand, would just get madder than a wet hen, and if Royce was the one who hit him, he would be looking for vengeance. I won't say for certain that he threw rocks without mud, but he very well could have.

Rubber Gun Fights

Besides our Chinaberry fights our other pastime was battling with "rubber guns". Those of you who have never experienced shooting a rubber gun, you may not know what they are. A good rubber gun would begin with an apple crate, which we could obtain free at Kirby's grocery in downtown Malakoff. Over the years, Eddie and I made lots of things out of these apple crates. Besides rubber guns, we also made our arrow shafts from the thinner boards. Years before, my Dad had used those apple crate boards to carve his creations with a pocketknife. The crate which originally contained apples, was a wooden box approximately 30" x 24", made of pine. The ends of the box were $1/2$" x 24" x 6" The bottom contained two boards approximately 1/8" thick, 30" long and 8" wide. The end boards were perfect for using a Coping saw to cut out a gun. There were several designs, but the most popular was made like a 45 gun. Next you would need a clothes pin, the kind with the spring in the middle. These pins would be "borrowed" from your family. After the gun was cut out, the clothes pin was attached with a "borrowed" shoestring or kite string. The longer the gun barrel the better because you wanted to be able to stretch the rubber band far enough to get a good pop. Next you needed an old bike inner tube so you could cut off a nice piece. The idea was to stretch the rubber band from the front of the gun barrel to the clothes pin and there you would open the clothes pin and clamp it with the rubber band. With the rubber band stretched out and tension on it, you now had your weapon. When you were ready to shoot your opponent, you merely squeezed the clothes pin, and the released rubber band went flying!! The ideal way was to have an ample supply of rubber bands, so you could quickly re-load. This game was all out war between our Southside members. You were supposed to shoot below the waist, at least that was the unwritten rule, but the truth was we shot anywhere we could. Those rubber bands would really sting, especially if you were hit in the face. There were many rubber gun designs; one in particular was the "machine gun" rubber gun. This required at least a 2 foot to 3 foot long 2" x $^1/_2$" wide board. About 10 notches were cut along the "barrel top" so that rubber bands could be stretched from the notches to the back end. Underneath the rubber bands a string was placed. Each rubber band could be shot as the string was pulled up. It wasn't until later on that we could actually buy large rubber bands in the store. These often came with the model airplanes and were used to wind up the propeller. They worked great with the rubber guns, but they were not as strong. A Rubber Gun battle might last for at least 30 minutes or until one side was eliminated or gave up. It was the most fun when we had at least four, but many times we didn't have four and with only two, the fight wouldn't last as long. Royce and Sammy, Eddie and I made four. Sometimes Rooster would join in, and one side would have an extra man. Royce, Eddie and I were about 4 or 5 years older than Rooster and Sammy, so we tried to even up the sides and many times Eddie and I teamed up against Royce, Sammy and Rooster. On occasion someone other than a Southside member might join us. As best I remember, Stanley (Red) Johnson sometimes joined the fray. I don't remember any of the girls ever being in our Rubber Gun fights or any other fights to that matter.

Sling Shots

Part of the fun we had was making our own stuff out of whatever was available. We used the Bike tubes to cut rubber bands for our rubber guns as well as using the rubber for our Sling Shots (of course we did not call them Sling Shots, but we used a term that would be offensive to many of my friends (N....Shooters). We meant no disrespect with this, but it was a commonly used term by everyone I knew. To us a Sling Shot was something entirely different, which I will later describe, but for now I will use the term Sling Shot to describe the instrument we made. The first thing to get was a nice Y shaped limb from a tree and next find and cut some rubber bands from the Bike Tube. The tongue from an old tennis shoe worked nicely for the pocket to hold the pebble. A groove was cut all around both tips of the Y so that the $1/4$ in. wide rubber band could be placed over the grooves and string wound around the rubber band holding it in place. Each Y would have a rubber band attached and then the tongue of the tennis shoe was tied to each. Back then there was only one kind of tennis shoe, made of canvas. They were all black and high tops. The tongue was used to make a pocket for holding a pebble. The fancy kind of Sling Shot (store bought kind) might have surgical rubber and either a wooden or metal Y. The pebble pocket for the homemade variety could also be cut out of a Bike tube. With our Homemade Sling Shots, we became pretty accurate and would often try to kill birds or other living things, but more likely we were only target practicing. Another way of making the Y instead of using a tree limb was to cut it out of an apple crate board. Instead of a Y, the cutout usually was a U shape with a handle.

What we referred to as an actual Sling Shot was like the one David used when he slew Goliath. Using this type Sling Shot was a little trickier than the so-called N Shooter. To make one you needed two strings that were strong with a piece of a Tennis Shoe tongue tied to the end of the two strings. The idea was to place the Pebble (rock) in the tongue and start swinging the entire thing in a circular arch as if you were winding up for a baseball pitch. This swinging or slinging gave the momentum that was needed to sling the rock forward. If one string was then released at the proper time, the rock would fly out in the direction you aimed it. It was tricky and required practice. Eddie and I did a lot of practice in the front yard because we had an ample supply of rocks that had been hauled in for our driveway. Directly across the street was an open field and houses were to the left and right. Miss Willie West's house probably caught an errant shot every now and then, but if so, she never said anything. What did happen was every now and then we would accidentally hit the electric wire that ran between electric poles or maybe even hit the transformer. When we did this, it was time to quit and hide out for a while. When timing was off that errant rock might end up anywhere, including going backwards into our own yard or maybe nearly striking a passing car. Once I mistakenly let go of both strings at the same time and that projectile soared across the road, along with my entire weapon. I was usually able to retrieve the Sling Shot, but once my Sling found the electric wire and with the momentum, wrapped itself around the wire and hung there.

Killing Birds

Of all the things the Southside Gang did, the one thing that I wish I could go back, and change is killing birds. From the first time I got my BB gun, I began a bird killing rampage. Eddie and I would often walk behind the Day's property where they had a very large pecan tree, and it was often filled with black birds. Several plots of ground would be plowed during the spring and birds would flock in. Sometimes the entire sky would almost seemed filled with black there were so many. They might be on the ground browsing the freshly plowed dirt looking for any morsel of food they could find, or they might perch high in that old pecan tree making a nice target. It was our sport to aim at the highest ones just to see if we could hit them. Much of the time, we did, and they would fall out of the tree, landing with a thud. Sometimes they would fly and often they were not even bothered by one of their own falling. As I recall, there were several different kinds of black birds. The regular black birds, the smaller cow birds and the ones we called black birds which were not blackbirds at all, but rather Starlings. After Eddie and I both graduated to shotguns, we might try shooting the whole flock as they grazed. I remember one time either Eddie or I one shot into the flock and nary a feather was hit. Those did fly off. Our favorite bird to shoot was what we called a BB bird because they were so dumb, we could shoot one, killing it, and the others would just sit there. We later learned that these were called cedar waxwings and they liked to sit in the China berry trees in our back yards and eat the ripened, fermented China berries. As they did so, they would become tipsy and make even better targets. They came in flocks and set in trees for a long time, giving Eddie and me plenty of target practice. At first, I had a lever action Red Ryder and later a Daisy pump BB gun. If we couldn't find a bird for a target, Eddie and I always found something, even some inanimate object like a tin can or an old bottle. We both became pretty good shots, and those poor birds didn't stand a chance. It was a completely stupid thing to do, and I am ashamed to say I killed as many birds as I could regardless of kind. Back of Eddie's land there was a row of trees that usually had birds galore. I could climb over my back fence, go over the back of the Day's property and there I would be near that row of trees. These trees are where we found our materials for our bows, so I suspect they were Iron wood trees. Another tree, which we called the Tickle Tongue tree, was the one Eddie and I liked to cut off a piece of the bark and touch it to our tongue. This would give us a Tickling sensation on the tongue. Like a lot of other stupid things we did, later we learned that this contained poison. We also learned Indians had used this tree bark to treat toothaches. This cluster of trees near the fence row is the spot where we first encountered those BB birds, and they were so close to us we could almost reach out to touch them. Eddie learned how to make a blow gun using a hollow fishing cane and a short piece of sharpened wire with cotton the exact size of the hollow cane. He was pretty adept at blowing on the 3 ft. long cane and sending that wire projectile out. One day a flock of BB Birds landed in his backyard and to this day I remember Eddie under the tree blowing his home-made blow gun and knocking out one those BB Birds, and none of the others even bothered to move. Beyond that row of trees was a large open field and we could see the Bartlett houses in the distance. Of the many times Eddie and I went into this field and shot at birds or something else, we never encountered anyone saying that we could not be there, so we kept going back. Royce, as far as I can remember, never hunted birds with us. Once Eddie and I were hunting in that open field and we saw a cotton tail rabbit at least 100 yards away just sitting there. I said to Eddie, "Watch me hit that rabbit!" Eddie said, "You can't hit that rabbit, it's too far away". I aimed several feet above the rabbit and fired. The next thing was that poor rabbit being hit and squealing loudly and in pain. We had to cut the poor thing's throat and kill it to get it out of its misery. Well, the good thing, it was meat for eating and so I did take it home and I had my Grandmother fry it for us. I am so sorry that I did this to the poor thing, now the only time I see a cotton tail is when I see one run over on the hwy. A rabbit's fur can be made into a good piece after it is removed from the rabbit and the rabbit has been gutted and prepared for eating. The skin is then stretched out and salted and cured. We did this with a lot of cottontail furs over the years. One thing we learned was an Old Wife's tale about R months. The only months to take a rabbit for eating purposes were during a month with an R in the name, like December for example. I think this had to do with colder weather. During the "wrong" months, when it was warmer, there would be "Wolf Worms" in the rabbit's back. These were parasites that embedded under the skin and appeared as knots. Back to the bird shooting stories.... Once Eddie and I were hunting in that back field, and I saw a dove at least 100 yards away, so I told Eddie, "Watch me hit that, Dove!!" "You can't hit that Dove, it's too far away!" But I did, square in the head. And then, I remembered, It is not dove season!! I think I buried that Dove and boy was I ever scared. Another time when it was dove season and I had a shot gun, I shot what I thought was a dove and it turned out to be a sparrow hawk. I think one pellet hit the poor little thing's wing. I decided to take it home and try and rehab the hawk. I placed it in my cage where I sometimes kept rabbits. It could not fly, so it needed time to heal and this way I could give it water and try to feed it. I tried different things to get it to eat, but to no avail. Finally, I decided to carry it back to the woods and let it go, which I did. Looking back on it, I should have tried to contact some animal rehab, but I doubt that there was anything like that back then, or at least not in Malakoff. Once while Eddie and I were roaming, we heard something that sounded like a woman screaming. This was a very distinct sound that made chills go up and down my spine. Finally, we saw the source of that screaming. Through the thick underbrush, there stood a large bird about the size of a Turkey or maybe bigger. We both identified that bird as a Pea Cock. I decided to chase it down. That was a mistake. I am surprised we didn't try to shoot it like we did everything else. I had a difficult time catching it, but as I did that sucker clawed the heck out me after I tried to grab hold. When I finally had the critter in hand, I walked home with it (along with nasty scratches on both arms)., thinking I had discovered a prize for our backyard. The same cage I used for the injured hawk became the holding place for that Pea Cock. South of the Day's property was a stand of woods which extended all the way to the road leading to the Bankston ranch. The Pea Cock belonged to them, and I had to return it. I can still hear that blood curdling scream in my mind, and I can almost feel those claw marks on my arms. When I graduated from BB guns to 22's I still liked to shoot birds or anything else that crossed my path. When we were in the 9th grade one of my classmates, James Newell, was a hunting buddy. He was not a Southside member, but a good friend. He lived on the East side of Hwy. 31, off a street to the North. James was an avid hunter as was I and we both were good shots with our 22's. The good thing about where he lived was the space available with not many houses around and so we could shoot without fear of hitting the wrong thing. One day he and I went on a bird killing spree. I remember shooting really tiny birds off the hi-line with perfect accuracy. Of course, I now regret doing this, but at the time it was more of a game to see which one could out-shoot the other. One of our targets just for practice was a peach seed on a fence post and accuracy was necessary for this task. From 50 feet away we both seldom missed. Our guns were single shot and we used 22 short bullets, so we had to reload each time. Another target that was more difficult was trying to light the head of a match sticking up from a fence post. Hitting the match was no problem, but being able to strike the match was. About every tenth shot we might strike it, but often it took more. This particular day was a Saturday, and we had hunted since early in the morning, killing blue jays, black birds, sparrows, chickadees, field larks and perhaps others. By afternoon we had killed over 100 between the two of us. Reflecting back on it, this was both pathetic and disgusting. That afternoon my Aunt and Uncle, along with future Southside members my cousins John and Sam Farrell came to pick me up. I can't remember how I carried the birds home, but carry I did and fed them to my cats. It has been more than 50 years since I have shot any birds other than game birds and I still to this day cringe every time I think about what I did. Now I have several bird feeders in the backyard and love watching all of my feathered friends, never ever thinking of harming one of them.

Dove Hunting

Along about the 1st of September Dove season would open and Royce would scoop up Eddie and I and we would head to the clay pits. There were many ponds around and Doves were plentiful. At least they were before the season opened. Somehow those birds knew when to get scarce. Late in the evening was the best time to hunt because doves would be coming in to get a drink or to feed along the banks. When we did go dove hunting, I am pretty sure Rooster and Sammy didn't go with us. They may have been too young, or another reason, we didn't trust them not to shoot one of us by accident. We each had a shotgun, Royce his double barrel 12 gage which we called long john, Eddie with his 12-gage pump and me with my 20-gage bolt action. As doves come flying in, they make a zig zag pattern and land with a flutter. We each learned early on that you need to lead the dove and swing your gun ahead as you followed the flight path. Sometimes just as you thought you had the bird in your sights and you pulled the trigger, the dove would zig zag and you would miss. The other problem was where the dove would fall. Some places might be inaccessible because it might land in a pond. If this happened, we would leave the kill there. We were not going to pull off our hunting clothes just to retrieve a single dove. Doves are dark meat and are very good eating, but you need to kill a few to have a mess. I am not sure what the limit was back then, but since we never bothered to have a hunting license anyhow, it didn't make any difference. As best I remember a box of 50 shells would cost about $1.50. I have not been dove hunting since the good old days of hunting with the South Side gang, so I really don't know what they cost now, but of course much more than $1.50 for a box of 50. Since Royce had the gun with the best range, he was able to fire away before Eddie and me. As per usual, Royce was able to out-do us. Dove hunting, like everything else, could be turned into a competition by Royce. The only time I was able to outshoot Royce was when I borrowed the old shotgun from my Uncle Edgar. This gun was a lever action shotgun probably made in the late 1800's. I had never before heard of a lever action shotgun, nor have I ever seen one since. It had originally belonged to my Great Grandpa Roberts, and I am sure he brought it with him when they came from Tennessee to Texas in 1897 via covered wagon. My Uncle Edgar obtained ownership of this gun after his Dad (my Great Grandpa) died. The progression of guns for me may have been the same for Eddie, but Royce had been using a gun much earlier than us. My sequence of guns was: should I include "cap pistols"?? Next, I advanced to "rubber-guns", Daisy Red Ryder BB gun, 50 shot pump Daisy, 22 single shot, and then 410 shot gun, single shot, then lever action 20 gage. Eddie and I were always shooting something: either an inanimate object like a tin can, bottle or anything alive, such as birds, rabbits, squirrels. We were both very good shots and although we did our share of killing birds, we tried to be safe with our hunting. When it came to hunting doves, it was for fun, but in addition we would have food. I don't remember the maximum number of doves that I ever killed at one time, but I doubt if it was any more than 3. Three would have made enough for a good meal. I remember once Royce invited our football coach, Bill Loggins, to go with us on one of our dove hunts. I think he also may have gone with us on one of our duck hunts, which is another story. It has been too long for me to remember what happened on either of these hunts, but the one thing I remember is that Coach Loggins was not only a good coach but also a good sport. Perhaps you could even say he was brave. During my 40 + years of teaching, I doubt that I would have gone on any kind of hunting escapade with my students. Perhaps I would have in my early teaching days, when I wasn't that much older than my students, but later I became more aware of what could happen. In case I didn't mention it, the doves we were hunting were Mourning Doves. We never saw any other type. I think white-tipped doves arrived much later. Remember, I said we had no hunting licenses. Back then if you hunted Doves in your own county, you didn't need a license. (Per Eddie Nokes in 2017...I asked him) Boy things have sure changed and as far as protection of the Dove population is concerned, for the good.

Ducks

One day while we were rambling in Paul Davis's jeep on the west side of Malakoff near Cedar Creek, Royce said he saw some ducks and he convinced us to return home, put on our warmest gear, and go back to where he thought they were. It was a cold day, drizzling and the temperature in the 30's with ice everywhere. Royce, Eddie, P.D. and I, equipped with our warmest clothes, socks, shoes, returned, all armed with shotguns. We spotted a flock in a slough about 100 yards away. We studied the situation, and the decision was made by Royce. The only way to get close enough to shoot was to crawl on our bellies. There was nothing to hide behind or to keep us from being seen. So, crawling we did, through an open field, breaking ice as we went. It didn't take that long I am sure, but it seemed forever, and it was very cold. I was starting to shiver but kept crawling. Of course, we weren't going to let Royce know we wanted to quit. When we got within about 25 or 30 yards those ducks flew, and we all shot. Not a feather was hit. You would have thought at least one of us would have a hit a duck. All we got out of this was icicles hanging off our clothes and Royce laughing. Another fine mess you got me in, Royce.

Crows and Banty Hens

As the Southside gang roamed the Walnut Creek area, looking for something.... anything to shoot, we often tried to shoot a Crow. We soon learned that crows are really smart and learned to quickly avoid us as we got too close. While on one of these outings Royce spotted a tree with a crow nesting. Since we had heard stories about crows making good pets, we thought this might be a good opportunity to capture one. Naturally it was Royce with the idea. "Hey, guys, we will never be able to catch one alive, so what if we got and egg and hatched it?" "That sounds good!!" we said. "But how do we do that?" Easy, Royce replied, "We climb the tree and retrieve and egg from the nest." "Who's going to do it?" we asked. "I will!" he said, and up the tree he went, climbing all the way to the top of that oak where the nesting crow set. The Cawing of the crows was ear splitting and somewhat unnerving, but not to Royce as he dodged the persistent attacking crows as they dived and pecked at him while trying to protect their nest. As I remember this incident, I can almost hear Royce laughing as he warded off those birds and his relentless quest to retrieve one of those crow eggs. Finally, he secured one of the eggs and then proceeded with the chore of getting down without breaking it. Royce was always up to any challenge, and this was no different. He placed the egg in his shirt pocket and carefully made his way down, as the crows dive- bombed him on his way, nipping at his back and head. He shrugged off these small pecks and eventually made it to ground level with the egg intact. The crows finally gave up and he showed us his prize; a whole crow egg about the size of a regular chicken egg, but not the color we were used to. So, now with the egg in hand, the next step is what to do with it and Royce had the answer. "We have a Banty hen now setting on eggs, so all we need to do is put this crow egg with her eggs and let her hatch it, then we can take care of the baby crow, feeding it and making it our pet." This plan sounded great, so that's what we did. It was not unusual to place a regular chicken egg among the Banty eggs when a Banty was setting. The chicken egg would hatch and though the chick would be somewhat larger, the Banty hen would have the same mothering instincts and consider this bigger chick part of her brood. There is one thing you need to remember: Baby chicks hatch with their eyes fully open and soon begin feeding on their own. A crow hatchling, like other birds, hatches with eyes closed and must be fed and nurtured by the parent crows. Either we didn't know this or had forgotten about it. In our minds, when it hatched, the mother Banty would take care of it. Each day we would take a look to see if any of the eggs were hatching and we kept a critical eye on that crow egg. Eddie, Rooster and I would be down at the Shelton's bright and early asking, "Hey, Royce has it hatched yet?" Royce replied, "No, not yet!!!" This went on for several days and then one day when we asked, Royce replied, "Yea, it hatched!!" We were all excited and exclaimed, "Really, that's great!!" "Yea, it hatched alright, but the Banty hen pecked and killed it!!" I guess our hen didn't think much of the Ugly Duckling story. Was the crow **too** Ugly??

Dynamite

The most dangerous game of all was definitely the one we "played' with Dynamite. I am sure today we would be arrested and charged as possible terrorists. During our Dynamite Adventures, I always tried to stay as far away from the dynamite as I could. It was Sammy who transported the article in a tow sack, along with the blasting caps. Looking back on this, it was Stupid with a capital **S!!** I have no idea how Royce originally obtained the cache and at the time I didn't want to know. I will give an educated guess which is probably the answer. We often swam in the body of water we called the Inch Pond, a deep pit formed by the Brick Yard excavating clay. That pit offered an excellent place to swim, and often we did so. I remember a small house about the size of an outdoor toilet found on the Brick Yard property. The entire area was an excavated hole covering several acres and within the large excavation is where the swimming hole was located. That little house had a padlock and we had previously suspicioned that dynamite was kept there. I don't know when or how the dynamite ended up in Royce's possession, but you can go figure. Our Southside Dynamite team consisted of Royce as the leader, Eddie and I as backup, Sammy carrying the Ammo and Rooster lagging behind. This was our usual Dynamite team as we walked to our destinations. Our goal was simple: use the dynamite to blow things up. When I reflect back on this, it is a miracle that we weren't killed or injured. The scenario of our Dynamite adventures all went something like this: Go to a place like the levee (which was farther South of town) and get set up to "fish". Though I remember parts of how we did this, I don't remember all. I would have run away from this, as would Eddie,

Rooster and maybe Sammy, but none wanted to be chastised by Royce and called chicken. I remember there was a large battery involved and wires that would connect the battery with the distant blasting cap. Dropping the dynamite with attached blasting cap and touching the wire to the battery would send the electric spark, igniting the blasting cap and the dynamite. The fish would then start rolling up and there was our catch for the day. Not only were we with illegal dynamite, our fishing was illegal also. By the way, I don't think any of us ever had a fishing license or a hunting license back then. (Not that you could get a license to fish this way) Our use of dynamite probably goes back to our early use of some other things we fished with (also illegal). The first that I recall was the use of the crank recovered from an old phone. When you cranked it, electricity was generated and if you had the connection to a wire running into the water, you could shock fish and they would boil to the surface. (F.Y.I. do not use an Aluminum boat, in fact don't try this at home or ANYWHERE ELSE!!) This was an easy way to catch fish and not nearly as destructive or dangerous as the dynamite. The alternative way was using Carbide. Carbide is a rock that when placed in water, produces Acetylene gas and years ago, the old miners, not having flashlights, would use Carbide lanterns or hats with a receptacle to house the Carbide. At the front of the hat was a disk-shaped reflective mirror and an opening for the gas to come out. Water was placed in with the carbide and when the gas came out it was lit and the metal reflected, giving a good light for the dark cave. Our method was simple. Use a quart-sized paint can, minus paint, with a lid that could be put securely in place. While in a boat, place water in the can, dump in some carbide, and quickly close the lid and drop it overboard.

The housed Acetylene gas would have no place to go, and the can would blow up, resulting in fish boiling up. This was not only fairly safe, but also, inexpensive, because, the railroad conveniently left us our ammunition. They used Carbide rocks to line the railroad ties.

Another story about dynamite comes to mind. I don't remember many, but this is one that I will not soon forget. This episode occurred on a warm January day when the usual South Side Dynamite Gang was on another adventure. Of course, Royce planned the outing. Eddie and I, Sammy, and Rooster tagged along with Sammy toting the ammunition. The sun was shining brightly, and it was much like a spring day. Royce decided that we should go to the Levee Break and do some "fishing", Southside style (You know with dynamite). As always, Royce had some challenge in mind, as the "fishing bait" (dynamite) was thrown into to the water while the five of us stood on the banks approximately 20-30 yards from where the "fish bait" landed. Royce said, "When the fish comes up after the bang, I will beat you to the fish!!" As I heard this, I was single minded in my thought. Royce was not going to beat me, so as soon as the fish boiled up, I quickly stripped to my skivvies and dived in, swimming as fast as I could to retrieve the floating fish. For once, I had beaten Royce!!! I grabbed that fish with great exuberance because at long last I had beaten Royce at something!! Then I realized, I was the only one in the water. About this time the cold of that water hit me!! It was a warm day for January, but that water was not!! This chill that hit me only was surpassed by the knowledge that on the banks of the levee, 4 clothed laughing hyenas were rolled over laughing at me. So, once again, Royce had won. I was not through freezing, that part had only begun. I did retrieve one fish, but I stood shivering on the banks, feeling rather persecuted to say the least. As usual Royce was laughing and so were the others. There stood Royce standing dry and warm on the bank, grinning from ear to ear and I knew I had been had! I can still feel that cold even today from some 60 + years ago, but the sting of the joke, perhaps even more. Ok, Royce, you win again!

The Inch Pond

One of the favorite hangouts of the Southside Gang was the Inch Pond. It wasn't always called this, but we began calling it that after Eddie and I started trying to fish in this clay pit. The only things we ever caught were very small bream about an inch or so long, thus the name: Inch Pond. We used the very smallest hooks available and as soon as the hook hit the water, we would get a bite. It was a lot of fun to catch those little suckers, and of course we threw them back in and probably caught the same one over and over. Prior to us calling it the Inch Pond it was simply "The Clay Pit", our favorite swimming hole. Eddie, Royce, Rooster, Sammy and I would skinny-dip here during the summer months. It was a great place to swim because the water was a clear aqua-blue and cool. Here we had mud ball fights, and all of the balls were free of any rocks. These mud balls were all pure clay, unlike the mud at the stock tank. Around the circumference was a sort of gray clay. This hole had been previously excavated to get clay for the Brickyard. It was often our strategy to try to touch bottom, which was impossible. The farther you went down the colder the water became, and as far as I was concerned it was bottomless. I don't know that anyone ever found the bottom, but judging from the material at the edge, we decided it had a lignite bottom. Malakoff had places where Lignite was mined back in the 30's although these spots were all on the North side of town. It was not unusual for us to spend 2- or 3-hours swimming and playing here and we liked to come here after we had done some other activity like hay hauling, football, basketball or something else that made us sweat. The Inch Pond was a great place to cool off. At the time we didn't think about it being dangerous, looking back on it, I know for a fact it was. We had heard stories of someone who drowned here years before, but we never knew the person. Of course, Royce would have reminded us that we were chicken if we had been afraid. At first my swimming consisted of more of a dog paddle and swimming in place trying to keep afloat, but during the summers when I visited with my Mother and Stepfather in Pt. Neches, my Stepfather taught me how to float. This feat was easier in the Gulf because the salt water buoyed me up. Nevertheless, I had learned some valuable skills that were used in the inch pond. I had learned how to float and how to hold my breath. Since we were trying touch bottom, we needed to hold our breath and we would practice near shore by diving under and holding our breath for as long as we could. We soon learned that if you let out your breath as your body cried for oxygen, you could stay under a little longer. Later I learned the reason. The CO_2 is actually what prompts your body to breathe and if you let your air out, you are blowing away carbon dioxide. I think I managed to hold my breath under water for perhaps 3 minutes or better. Again, Royce made a game of this. He and Eddie would both beat me holding their breath, but I could beat Rooster and Sammy. What I didn't know until years later, there were eyes watching us. From the Inch Pond we could see the Bartlett house, which was way up on a cliff perhaps 300 yards away. Vicki Lewis was there visiting the Vermilions (Tony and his two brothers) and she would watch us from her vantage point. If I had known this at the time, I would have been too embarrassed to skinny-dip. By the way, I think we probably kept our undershorts on at least sometimes. One thing I am reminded of that should be mentioned. My Grandmother did not know that I was swimming in the clay pits, AKA Inch Pond, or she would have been "fit to be tied" Sadly, recently I learned that the Malakoff Clay Company filled in that Old Inch Pond. Now many of our fond memories lie buried, but not forgotten.

Tops and School Yard Games

I remember in grammar school we had recess, and this was when we would go to our Malakoff Elementary School playground. In the playground we had a choice of the Merry Go Round, Seesaw, Monkey bar, slide or swing. The Merry Go Round was lots of fun because you got to spin around in a circle, get dizzy and jump off. One of the problems came when you tried to get on while it was spinning. This was especially true when some of the bigger kids would try to intimidate you and keep you from getting on. This always happened to me because everyone was bigger than I. Even the girls were bigger. As I remember it, all of the girls were taller than the boys or at least many were. The girls at this age were also faster. Yet another playground game was that of racing on foot. Don Bierd and I were the two smallest, and everyone delighted in picking on us, especially Jax Baird who was the biggest kid in our 3rd grade class. Another neat trick that the bigger kids used was with the see-saw. The bigger kids would delight in letting me or Don sit on one end of the seesaw and them on the other. They then would hold us up in the air because they outweighed us about two to one. If they set all the way to the end, we had no chance to balance. We quickly learned about levers, which is what a seesaw is. If Jax or Eddie was on the very end, I would always be suspended no matter where I sat. On the other hand if they chose to move toward the center and I all the way to the end, we could balance and could See-Saw. This wouldn't last long because soon Jax or Eddie and sometimes Ronnie Stockman would move so that I would be lifted way up and then they would jump off leaving me crashing to the ground receiving a good butt whacking. I soon learned that I didn't like the see-saw. The good thing about swings is that you for the most part could control how high you would swing. This sometimes was altered by some smart alec who would shove you as hard as they could and then you would swing up really high. They would keep swinging you until the arc you inscribed was quite large. There you were trapped in the swing and the only thing you could do was wait until the oscillation of the pendulum wore down or the more dangerous way.... jump out. I remember one time I did choose to jump out and I did so backward, landing on my chin. It is a wonder I didn't break my neck. The most swing arch was accomplished when you stood up in the swing and tried to generate as much height as you could obtain and then jump out. A less dangerous piece of equipment was the monkey bars, which I had less trouble with. Monkey Bars consisted of a ladder-like design parallel to the ground and a perpendicular ladder to climb. Once you reached the first rung, the idea was to grab the first bar with one hand and then the other. At this point you would be hanging with your legs dangling. I believe there were about 10 rungs that you had to move across one at a time, reaching with one hand, grabbing the next bar and pulling yourself along until you reached the other side. Though I could do this at times, I often only made a few bars before my strength gave out. This was not a fat person's forte because their weight would be too great for them to lift their own body. One had to be strong and agile to do this and at this age I was neither. I think we were given about 15 minutes to be out and about playing on the equipment. Sonny Humphries and I were close to the same size, and we became buddies. Once he talked me into crossing the short rock fence at the back of the playground and going to his house. His house was only a short distance away, just the right distance to get us in trouble. We didn't do that again. We were only threatened with that Electric Paddle Mr. Lawson kept in his office, but the threat of that imagined paddle was enough to scare us. Shows how naïve we were. As we got older our activities during recess changed. One I remember was an exercise conducted by Mr. Lawson for the boys of all grades. I am not certain if all grades of boys were included, but I remember Don Bierd and I were the ones picked on again. More than likely we were in the 3rd grade. The exercise was a gauntlet. You know, like the Indians used in some of their initiations and tortures. Every boy pulled off their belt and two rows of boys were formed. The idea was for the boy at the end to run through the two rows as each boy in the row got a swat at your behind. As you dashed through the line, getting your licks, you then assumed you place at the front, where you would get to swing your belt as each person tried to pass. This game was great for the fast kids, but not for the slower ones, which I was. One thing I quickly learned if you didn't want to get hit multiple times by the same person, you move through the gauntlet as quickly as you could. Can you imagine this being allowed today???

After we entered High School, (my 1957 Graduating class was the last 8$_{th}$ grade class housed in high school), our games changed. It was no longer recess, but we were given a 30-minute activity period. Out by the bus barn two of our games were horseshoe tossing and washers. The game Horseshoes was played with real horseshoes, not the manufactured like today. Washers were played with washers the size of a silver dollar. A hole was dug deep enough to sink a tin can into the dirt. The chosen can was just big enough for the washer to fit snugly if you were lucky enough to get a ringer. With the horseshoe game, the terms leaner brings to mind a statement...Close only counts in Horseshoes and Hand grenades.

Our other game was playing Tops...During activity period we would gather near the bus barn for our Top tourney. A circle with a diameter of approximately 3 or 4 feet was drawn in the hard clay soil. The next step was to spin your top in the circle and the group outside the circle would get a chance to throw their top at some spinning top in the middle. If their top knocked out a top spinning in the middle, the person outside the circle who threw the top got to keep the top that was knocked out. My big problem at first was that I didn't know how to spin a top. A top is made of wood about the size of a golf ball, maybe a little bigger, with a pointed end where a metal spike is inserted. I'll have to show you a picture of one because I am having a difficult time trying to describe one. The way to spin a top is to wrap a string around the top and draw it tight, twisting the string completely around all the way to the spike. There are two ways to toss the top, one holding the top upside down and the other right side up. When I first started, I couldn't do either. If one tosses it correctly it will spin until its momentum stops or it is hit with another top. I had to rely on my granddad to show me how to spin my top. I practiced at home on our wooden front porch. This was not that good of an idea, because our porch had grooves which the top could fall into, and also, the spike would make indents in the porch, which my Grandmother did not like. Now that you have an idea of what Top spinning is about, I will give you the poem that I wrote for my good friend Eddie. I wrote this 50 years after we had flung our tops toward our friends' tops. As many as 10 or 15 boys may have gathered around that circle trying their best to knock out a spinning top. So here is that poem.

ODE TO EDDIE'S TOP
By Don Henderson

The tops that once we played with as kids
Spun out of control in little circles, up for hits
And of course we'd plug 'Em mighty fast
Those left standing, how did they last?

Big ones, little ones, old ones, new ones, every size shape and spin,
Were clobbered, agin and agin.
How did you spin yours? Was it upright or upside down?
Or did you just spin it whatever way you wound?

What fun as a kid to spin one's top,
Escaping that circle or being a flop.
Hours we spent, spinning those things
I'll bet you remember those tops and dirt-rings.

Sometimes at "Activity" period
In school, out by the gym
We were driven to knock our buddy's top on the rim
Spin your top, see if you could last
Everyone else tried to nail your top, and fast.

My poor little top has been injured sore,
But it still kept spinning round some more.
Four more tried to strike it without luck
It wiggled and waggled and was struck,
But stayed to spin again this sitting duck.

Oh, little top how hard to learn your spin it took,
Hours of winding string and chores and study forsook.
Wind and spin a flop would go,
Could not get that little top to show.

Then one day, Eddie's top was spun,
I knocked that sucker out of the circle in round one.
That top was mine to keep,
Those were the rules, my heart did leap!!
Finally, I spun that top with one right spin!!
Oh, boy I knocked that top right out of the pen!!

Would that Top would never flop
But if indeed, it does in time,
Flop, Flop, His, His,
Oh what a relief it is, His, His
Not Mine

These are pictures of my tops showing their battle scars.

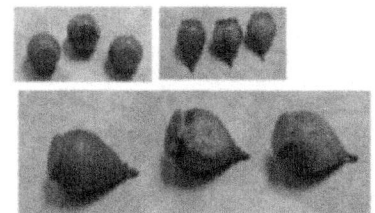

Apple Core, Apple Core,
Who's Your Friend

This was another game we played. If someone brought an apple to school, the first thing was to twist the stem off and as you twisted, you repeated the alphabet, a, b, c, d, etc... The letter when the stem came off was the first letter of your girlfriend's/boyfriend's name. I suppose some cheated, while others just dreamed.

The "Apple Core, Apple Core, who's your friend?" was used on the playground. After the apple was eaten down to the core and the phrase repeated, a "friend" was chosen and then the apple core was chunked at said "friend". "Friend" was a misused term and had more to do with whomever the person wanted to attack. The friend could end up with an apple core striking them square in the face or some other part of the body. The size of the thrower often determined whether the one being hit would retaliate. Often tempers flared, but most of the time the person getting hit just waited for the time to get revenge and took it with their own core chunk.

School Pranks

School pranks were common in our classroom. Some of this had begun back in elementary school. I never knew who put that rubber eraser in the stove when we were in Miss Annie Pope's class. This happened in the 6th or 7th grade in Malakoff Grammar School. I strongly suspect it was Kenneth Willingham. Kenneth had moved to Malakoff from Ft. Worth and was living with his Grandparents, Dewey and Pearl Dodson. Kenneth and Miss Annie Pope had locked horns on more than one occasion, and I suspect, Kenneth used this as retaliation. Of course, there were several others who had "clashed" with Miss Annie Pope, so it might have been any one of them. The smell of that burning rubber eraser was gross, and Miss Annie Pope attacked the problem, but not to anyone's satisfaction. She asked for the person responsible to step forward, and when there were no volunteers and she asked if any of us knew who the culprit was. If any did, we weren't telling. Those who were students at the Old Rock School in Malakoff will remember our source of heat came from the radiators that ran along the side near the windows. I can almost smell those burnt eraser fumes to this day. Miss Annie Pope's solution was to close all the windows and the door and allow us to sit and smell that awful smell irradiating from the radiator. I am sure she would have been fired or at least reprimanded if she had done something like this in 2017. There we were trapped, not only the dirty dog who did the deed suffered, we all did. Thank God, the same act never happened again. The real danger to such a prank and the reaction to it cannot be overstated. Who knows which of us may have been physically affected? She finally opened the windows to air the place out. Eddie and I were the only two South Side members in our class, although our neighbor

Sallye Dodson might also be considered because she did play football with us until she began her womanhood. We could also count our neighbor Henry Allen as a Southside member, but because of the problems he had with his eyes, he never went with us on any hunts, so I would list him as an honorary member. Sometimes he did come over and shoot baskets with us in Eddie's front yard. Eddie, Henry or I were never the ones pulling the pranks, nor was Sallye. I am not sure who the culprits were who pulled other pranks. I do have my suspicions though. Ronnie Stockman comes to mind when I reflect back on our 8th and 9th grade class. We had several mischievous boys in our class and any one of them could have been guilty. Kenny Andrews or Bo Johnson both were known to take part in a few tricks. I am not going to say that I was completely without guilt nor was Eddie. After Crossroads joined our group in the 9th grade, we added another trickster.... Buster Carter. The most common prank was Spit Wads, which the perpetrator would create by chewing on a piece of notebook paper until it was a nice and spit juicy. Then he would roll it and fold it so that it would fit nicely onto a rubber band. Suddenly while the teacher's back was turned, splat a spit wad would hit you in the head. If the teacher left the room for any length of time this might turn into an all-out war with spit wads flying everywhere. Another of the dangerous pranks one of our dear classmates contrived was the "pin cushion". The pin cushion was constructed by rolling a piece of paper into a ball and then sticking straight pins all around so that the sharp points protruded. After sitting on one, it became common practice for me to look closely before sitting. Even this "head's up" didn't stop some of our dear friends' tricks. They would roll it under just as you set down and you would get a pin in your butt. Someone once put a Pin

Cushion in the teacher's seat before he came to class. I think it may have been our 9th grade Algebra Teacher Mr. Pierce. We called him Shemp because he parted his hair in the middle and had a striking resemblance to one of the three stooges named Shemp. Anyhow, we knew what the person had done, and we all waited patiently for him to sit down and receive his reward. Shemp was not my favorite teacher, which I will later explain, but he didn't deserve this. He came in and set down. We anticipated an immediate response, but instead, he only set there and began the class. I never knew, nor did anyone else, if he even felt it. If he did, he never let on. He either had a very tough butt or maybe thick pants. If anyone had a reason to do this to Mr. Pierce it would have been me, but it was not I. The reason I might have wanted to do this was because of an incident which occurred previously. Sitting directly behind me was one of the girl Southside members, my cute little neighbor Sallye Dodson. My first interest in the opposite sex began to demonstrate itself during the early days of my 9th grade. One day, I was turned around talking to Sallye while Mr. Pierce was trying to teach Algebra. I am sure he asked me to turn around, probably more than once. Either I didn't hear him or pretended not to. All of a sudden, he threw a chalk eraser and hit me in the back. This was my first and only encounter with the paddle. Mr. Larkin was called, and I was escorted to the hall and given a swat, which I deserved. What I didn't deserve was the eraser being thrown at me and this is what my Grandmother took issue with. She was at school as soon as she learned of the incident. The swat she understood, just not the eraser. I usually was a model student, but not this time.

Another dangerous trick was a dart made with a match, pin, and paper. The dart was constructed by taking a match and inserting a straight pin in the very end. The head of the straight pin was then cut off leaving a sharp point. On the opposite end of the match, a carefully cut slit was made and paper was inserted to function like wings. It is a wonder that someone didn't get an eye put out. The idiot that did this would toss the dart at someone's back and it would stick through their clothes, giving them a sting and in some cases, they had to pull the dart out of their skin. I don't remember any girls doing this or getting nailed, but they might have. I know who the culprit was, but all I will say right now it was NOT a Southside member. I am sure there were other pranks, many of which I didn't even know about, but there is one I definitely remember. I suppose you could call it a prank, or you might say it was just another stupid escapade of teenagers. Eddie and I were seniors and we both chewed tobacco, either Day's Work or Beechnut, which was the chew-choices of our day. The last period was our Senior English class with Ms. Cartlidge, followed by football practice. The exit leading to our dressing room was a short distance from our class. Eddie and I would have our mouths full of tobacco juice needing to spit. Where to sit in the class became somewhat of a dilemma. If we set up front, the chance of getting caught was increased, but sitting at the back gave a longer dash to the back door. Why we Eddie and I were not caught still remains a mystery.

The Board of Education

If you misbehaved when I was in elementary school, you might be headed for a paddling, which we called the Board of Education. Two or three swats applied to one's rear were enough to deter most students who were acting up. It was quick, easy and efficient. There was none of the modern-day suspensions for minor offenses, nor were you sent to an Extension School. In our elementary school, everyone knew in Mr. Lawson's (the Principal) office was that dreaded electric paddle, which we all feared. The mere thought of this kept most of us in line. On occasion some boy (girls never really were troublemakers) would do something minor like maybe keep on talking when the teacher asked them to be quiet. After due warning, Mr. Lawson might be called or perhaps the teacher would escort the misbehaving student to the hall and administer a couple of swats. There was no such thing as prescribing drugs for hyper students to keep them quiet. Usually, a couple of swats to the behind got their attention. I avoided any swats, not only for the fear of that electric paddle, but also the fear of the beating I would get at home when my Grandmother heard of my misbehavior. It wasn't until high school when my algebra teacher and I did not see eye to eye and my incessant talking resulted in my first and only swats. The most memorable paddling incident that comes to mind involved one of our honorary Southside members, Stanley "Red" Johnson. Mrs. Richards was up in front of Red's class using one of those paper cutters. You know the one with the "guillotine-like" blade. She said, "'Uh, I hope I don't get my finger caught in this!" Red, in the back of the room, whispered, "I hope she gets her head caught in it!!" and Mrs. Richards heard him. This was the wrong thing for Stanley to say because Mrs. Richard's husband was the principal. It was reported that Red's rear end was black and blue after Mr. Richards finished administering the paddling. This was way overboard and probably resulted in the Richards not being rehired.

Tony Vermillion, my friend one grade behind me, received the Board of Education for a minor infraction, but it got everyone's attention. If you are going to be smart-alecky you just might get a swat or two. His swats resulted from his response to his English teacher's question about William Shakespeare. The class assignment had been to read a certain English book section which included facts about Shakespeare. Mrs. Cartlidge asked Tony, "Tony, how did William Shakespeare rank in English literature?" Tony either had not read the section or was being a smart-alec. He answered, "Well, he was pretty rank!!" This answer earned him a swat or two. These minor offenses were quickly taken care of, and the sting of that paddle was a lasting reminder not to be a smarty pants. The more severe the infraction the more swats given.

I began my teaching career at Hartman Junior High on the East side of Houston in 1962 and there was one student who constantly misbehaved. In those days every teacher kept a paddle nearby and I suppose I had one. The rule required the teacher have a witness and then swats could be applied while in the hall. In my almost forty years of teaching, I used the paddle a grand total of twice, both on this very same student. In his case, I don't believe it did any good and that is more than likely why I never used this type of discipline again. The interesting thing about this student, here I was a country boy from Malakoff in the big city of Houston and here this big city boy, Jack Cook, not only had relatives in Malakoff, but later moved there. His grandfather was a Jackson from Malakoff. He and I became good friends after we found this out. Small world, isn't it?

Later in my teaching career, paddling became controversial. Some parent would declare, "You can't paddle my kid!", so you could only paddle those whose parent gave permission for paddling. Eventually paddling was eliminated altogether and I truly believe this was a big detriment for education. If the paddle was applied in the early grades, by the time a student reached high school, they had usually shaped up. If no paddling was used in elementary school, by the time a student got to high school it was too late to paddle.

My 39 Chevy Coup

Old Blue, the Blue Buzzard, my 39 Chevy was appropriately named because of its hand-painted blue color. The previous owner had used a brush to paint the '39. There was no evidence of any spray painting. I acquired old blue when my Grandmother befriended a woman whose husband died. Suspicion of foul play was even rumored. Some even suggested the befriended woman may have done him in. The man had worked for Tanner's as a mechanic and when he died, his children apparently decided they wanted this wife out of his house and so she came to stay with us. Bill Norville was the mechanic's name, and his suspected wife was Mary Jo Norville. (Just as a side note Mary Norville was listed as a beauty shop customer in my Grandmother's 1939 scrapbook, so my Grandmother had known her from the past). I believe this was about 1955 or 56. We paid her $50 for that car and boy I wish I still owned it because it would be worth a bunch. Mary Jo Norville stayed with us for several months, bringing with her numerous pieces of furniture and other things into our already cluttered and crowded home. Not sure why my grandmother did this, but she did. The old '39 was really only about 16 years old, but at the time; I thought it was really old. Considering that I now drive a 13-year-old car, the '39 wasn't all that old. The day I first drove that car, I will never forget. Eddie agreed to go with me when I took it out south on Crossroads drive. He may not have ever gotten into the car had he known what was about to transpire. Because I was an inexperienced driver a wild ride took place. The car had a vacuum shift with the gear shift on the steering wheel and to change gears you needed brute strength and even then, the gears would grind. Luckily in those days, there was not much traffic to deal with, but there was enough that I should not have driven on this road without more experience. As we sailed along, going maybe 45 mph along the winding, hilly road, I experienced no problems, nor did I see another vehicle. Meanwhile, Eddie set quietly, I think too scared to move, much less say anything. The next thing I remember was seeing the road that I needed to turn on, but coming out on that road was a school bus. I was not experienced at applying brakes in a reasonable fashion to negotiate a turn, so when I made the right-hand turn, I was going at least 40 miles per hour trying to turn onto a dirt road. The dust was flying, the tires squealing, my heart pounding and Eddie gripping that car seat as if his life depended on it. .... perhaps it did. As we skidded around that corner, Lord only knows how I missed that bus. As soon as I could I pulled over and stopped for a long pause. Eddie just looked at me with a sheepish grin on his face and said, "Boy, that was close!!" and it was. Another time the good Lord and his Angels were watching out for us. I nervously drove back home, parked the car and didn't drive it again for several days. Eddie quickly exited as soon as we arrived in my driveway and hurriedly trotted next door to his home, baring possibly wet pants.

Sometime later, when I had become a little more experienced, I drove up to the Shelton's. The Shelton's lived on a hill south of us and east of the Crossroads highway. To reach their house you had to traverse a 200-yard single car gravel path. At the top of the hill, a white wooden fence surrounded the house. On this day, Royce and I.V. (his Dad) were in their yard at the top of the hill. I can't remember why I went to visit, perhaps to show off my car. This episode I remember as if it happened yesterday. After I had rolled down the window and talked to Royce and I.V., I decided to back out. I couldn't back all the way down the drive, but there was space to my left to back into. As I backed up my front bumper hung on a fence post. As I tried to figure my next move, I remember

Royce and I.V. were now almost rolling on the ground, laughing at me. I finally figured how to extricate the bumper, but not the red face of embarrassment. Of course, the news of Don's driving soon filled the neighborhood air waves, which of course was by word of mouth. It was often said about Malakoff, "If you spit in your backyard, by the time you went back in the house, what you did would be all over town." Years later, Royce would snicker and remind me of it.

Incidents with the Blue Buzzard didn't stop here, there were more to come. It was my habit to come flying into my Grandmother's yard with Old Blue, heading directly toward our house. Of course, I would apply the brakes and stop well beyond the house. I had done this on many occasions without incident. One day I came flying in as usual, applied my brakes and ...nothing. No time to think, I quickly threw Old Blue into reverse and that car stopped on a dime!! If it had not, I would have ended up on our front porch. Thank you, Lord, once again!!! Still shaken from that experience, I suddenly realized, "What if I ruined the transmission??" As I pondered this question, I knew that until I checked the brakes, I couldn't try the transmission. The brakes just needed brake fluid, and luckily, nothing was wrong with the gears. This slowed me down and from then on when I entered the yard it was at a much slower pace.

Once the Blue Buzzard's battery quit working and so I devised a method to bypass this. The older cars all had a standard transmission and could be started by pushing the car to get it moving while in neutral, turning on the key, engaging the clutch, putting it in gear while holding down the clutch, then popping the clutch. At this point if you had enough momentum, the car would start. Since I didn't drive at night, so I didn't need a battery for lights, nor did I drive very far. This starting method was all I needed to get me going. My ingenious idea I developed so I wouldn't need to buy a battery was to park parallel in front of the house heading south. The road was flat here for maybe 20 or 30 feet, and then 200 yards farther a downhill began. At the end of the hill the road curved right and another downhill with an even greater incline. I had this procedure down to a science. This was my sequence: roll down the window, turn on the ignition, reach in through the window and steer. While I was steering through the window, I was also, shoving and getting up enough momentum to get me past that first 20 feet so that I could have a downhill. As I ran along beside the car with my arms through the window steering, I would jump onto the running board. The next step was to open the door quickly, jump into the car, pop the clutch and like clockwork, the engine would crank, and off I would go. I did this for several weeks, repeating the exact sequence without a hitch. Then one day still with no battery and Old Blue parked at the front of our house I decided to start Old Blue, once again using the same sequence as I had done for the past several weeks. I rolled down Blue's window, stuck my arms through and turned on the key. Then I began shoving her off so as to get a running start. I jumped onto the running board and as I had done before, I then started to open the door. It would not open!! By now I had reached that first hill and Old Blue was steadily increasing speed. I desperately clung to that steering wheel through the window, steering down that hill with my heart racing. The door would not open. As Old Blue began racing down that hill my heart was racing even faster and there to my frightened eyes was that sharp curve. Coming from the opposite direction was an 18-wheeler. Steering around that curve was difficult for me when in the driver's seat, but now that I was on the running board, it was even more difficult. It seemed like forever, but when you are clinging for dear life on a moving vehicle, time seems to fly by like a fog and so does the mind. With all my strength and agility, I tried the door again and praise the Lord it opened!! Quickly I entered the car, guiding it while in the driver's seat, popped clutch and she started. I cannot remember ever being as scared as I was while clinging like a bug in a windstorm, trying to keep the car in line. Needless to say, I was so scared, my knees were shaking and even after I stopped the car it probably took another hour for me to calm down. I drove back to the house and never ever started Old Blue again by shoving her down the hill. A new battery was bought, and a solemn oath given to never park the blue buzzard on that hill with the intention of starting it by pushing. Again, thank you Lord and your Angels!!

There were several other adventures, or perhaps, misadventures with the Blue Buzzard, but the one which really stands out in my mind occurred after a football game. If you don't know the design of a '39 Chevy, you need to know in order to appreciate this story. The hood was designed so that either the passenger side or the driver's side could be lifted. There was a mechanism or handle that needed to be turned to open either side. In order to lock the hood down, the reverse turn was made. So, instead of being able to lift the hood in one piece as modern cars do, it was designed to lift one side at a time. After the football game, my buddy and teammate, Neil Williams and I took our dates on a ride past Neil's house. Neil's house was the same ranch the Bankston's had previously owned, but now it belonged to the Williams. This night was very cold, maybe in the 30's and the wind was howling to beat sixty. Neil was in the back seat with his girl and my girl set up front. Our intentions were to go to a well-known parking place and do a little smooching, but this was not to be. Fate had other plans. As I drove along, anticipating our soon to be romantic interlude, all of a sudden, a big wind came blowing by and Old Blue's hood lifted off in one piece and I swear I saw it flapping like a big bird in my rearview. I immediately stopped as soon as I could and then Neil and I had to retrieve that hood which had taken flight. Together we managed to get the hood back on and as far as I could tell there wasn't much damage done to the hood. The damage was with our plans, which were kaput for the night. Any country boy from that day and time will tell you, a supply of baling wire was always carried, and this is what we used to temporarily re-secure the hood; but alas, we could not re-secure our romantic intentions. Embarrassed, cold and romantically unfulfilled, our dates were taken home and as far as I remember, Neil and I never doubled dated again. A short time later my Granddaddy Tom saw me, and he knew who I had been dating. Granddaddy Tom, said, "Son, you know that gal you've been dating is your cousin!!" "What??" "No!!" Well, that ended my dating with that girl, not that she would have gone out again with me anyway after that Blue Buzzard episode. It didn't take long for the wagging tongues to spread the story and so by the time school began on Monday, everyone in the entire school knew exactly what had happened. They had previously made fun of the Blue Buzzard anyway and now they had more ammunition.

My Aggie Trip with Royce

Royce Wayne Shelton Breaks Hand In Grid Practice At A & M

Royce Wayne Shelton, who is attending Texas A&M at College Station suffered a broken left hand in football practice the past week.

Royce is a member of the Freshman squad, receiving the injury when his hand was caught in a helmet of one of the players on the opposing team.

He was treated at the College hospital, where his hand was put in a cast for six weeks. Doctors say he will not be able to work out with the team for the remainder of the year.

In 1956 Royce had been given scholarship to play football for Texas A&M. The head coach that year was the fabled Bear Bryant, who the year before had taken the Aggies to the infamous Junction camp. Those survivors were Royce's teammates. 1956 was a great year for the Aggies. They were 9-0-1 during the regular season. UNDEFEATED, tarnished only by a tie. The Aggies lost the Gator Bowl game to Tennessee 3-0 but finished the 1956 season 5th in the final poll and John David Crow was the Heisman trophy winner. The Freshmen Aggies, which Royce was one, did not play with varsity and had their own schedule. Early in the year Royce had an injury as reported in this article. According to the article, Royce broke his hand when it was caught in the helmet of an opposing player and his hand was put in a cast for six weeks. He was not able to work out with the team for the remainder of the year. This injury, as well his poor academics, spelled the end of his Aggie career. Royce finished his college playing days at Stephen F. Austin.

During the early part of January 1957, Royce begged me to go back to College Station with him. He had earlier written a letter, asking me to visit with him, and as old Southside gang member, I really wanted to take him up on his invite, but it was likely my Grandmother would not have been keen on the idea. I was a Malakoff High School senior, and Senioritis had set in big time. It certainly sounded like a great opportunity for me to get away from high school for a while. A trip to Texas A&M and a Turkey Day game sounded cool. The first letter Royce wrote was an offer for Eddie and me to join him for the annual

Aggie/Longhorn football game. By the way, the Aggies won that year!! This letter was written, Friday, November 23, 1956. The original letter, which I have kept all these years, is shown here. My Grandmother must have seen the letter because she made note on Royce's envelope about a Beauty Shop appointment. (She wrote: **Mrs. Ingram wanted a set Monday**). I will give you a complete transcript of this letter, so you can see for yourself what he wrote.

Neither Eddie nor I went to this game and my memory as to why is lost. I suspect it had a great deal to do with his parents and my Grandmother nixing the trip. Later Royce came home for Christmas and that is when he talked me into going back to College Station with him. More will be said about this after I give you the transcript of this November letter.

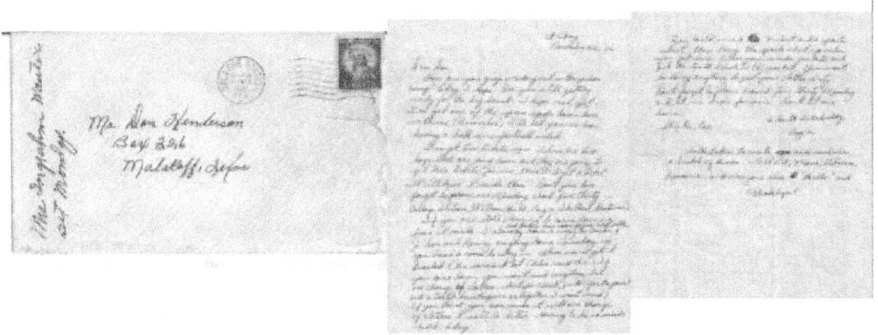

The following is a transcript of that letter.
Friday, November 23, '56
Dear Don, How are you guys making out in the prison camp? Okay, I hope. Are you still getting ready for the big break I hope not yet. I've got one of the spare rods down here with me (Remember!) I'll bet you've been having a

ball since football ended. **NOTE: THE ("RODS") PROBABLY WERE THE STICKS OF DYNAMITE……. SEE THE STORY ABOUT DYNAMITE) I've** got two tickets, now. There are two boys that are going home, and they are going to get their tickets for me, then I'll get a ticket. We'll have it made then. Don't you two forget to phone me Monday about five thirty-College Station, Walton Hall, Royce Shelton (that's me) If you are still planning to come down, we have it made. I already have a way to Austin and Dickie has room for us Wed. nite. J. Don and Benny are going home Tuesday, so you have a room to stay in. Thurs we've got it knocked. (Be sure and let Eddie read this) If you come down you won't need anything but one change of clothes, shirt, pair of socks, pants (for the game) and a tooth brush (apiece or together, I won't mind) If you think you can make it with one change of clothes it will be better, having to do so much hitch hiking. You could wear a T-shirt and a sports shirt, then hang the sports shirt up when you get here. Wear your suede jackets and put the toothbrush in the pocket. You won't be doing anything to get your clothes dirty. Don't forget to phone around five-thirty Monday and let me know for sure. Don't let me down.

Write too   A South Side Buddy, R o y c e

Tell Lokie to write and send me a bushel of kisses. Tell Ed, Mom, Thesea, Sammie, and everyone else "Hello" and "Goodbye!"

This letter was written in November, near Thanksgiving. I am guessing Royce came home during the Christmas holidays, which would have been in late December. The usual break back then was to have 1st semester finals after the Christmas break. It was during this vacation period that Royce enticed me to hitch-hike back to College Station with him. He explained he had only one college course he could pass and that was English. The plans were to thumb our way back to A&M and he would study for his final and then after he took it, we would return to Malakoff, VIA our thumbs again. With the plans made, we left on a Thursday. High school vacation had ended for me, and I was back in school. This likely was January 1957 just after New Year's. In order to go with Royce, I had to skip Friday's classes. How I did this without my Grandmother's permission (or with her permission) is still a mystery. My good friend and football teammate, Kenneth Carrol, was my unofficial campaign manager for Student Body President. We were having elections for president that Friday, but one candidate (me) would not be there. Ken Carrol had organized and posted many signs encouraging people to vote for Don Henderson (me) One read, "GET ON THE BAND WAGON, VOTE FOR PEDRO (my nick name)" Another read, "I'LL BE HANGED IF I DON'T VOTE FOR PEDRO". You must under-stand that for Malakoff High School, this was a big deal at the time. In fact, it was announced that this was Malakoff High School's first student body election. Later we learned this was not true. The first elected president was Raymond Reese in 1942. So, I left the race up to the voters and went with Royce. It was so hotly contested that I can't even remember who my opponents were, if any. Upon my return to school Monday, after my Aggie trip, I was greeted with, "You are the new Student Body President", which came as one of the biggest surprises that I ever remember. How this happened, I don't know. I suspect the way the election was run, each class, 9th-12th had a meeting and each class voted by show of hands. This was the way that all elections were done. When class favorites were picked, the persons nominated went into the hall and the class voted by show of hands. Upon returning to the classroom, it was announced who was elected most Handsome, Most Beautiful, Most Likely to Succeed and etc. Since I was not there, I obviously did not go into the hall, but I figure this was the way I was elected. I will talk more about my Presidential term later. Meanwhile, Royce and I left on Thursday afternoon. Most of the memories and details are long lost from my memory bank and since Royce is no longer on this Earth, I can't ask him, so I must reconstruct what happened with some imagination. I do remember it was cold and rainy, typical January weather. College Station is approximately 150 miles from Malakoff and traveling at the speed limit at that time, which was 60 mph, it would take us about $2\,^1/_2$ hours to make the trip. Hitch-hiking was different. You had to catch someone traveling in the right direction and hope they were heading toward your destination. I know we had to travel to Corsicana on highway 31 and then take highway 75 (This was 1957 and I-45 was not yet built). From there I am not sure exactly how we went, nor what kinds of rides we were able to get. What I do remember, we did arrive at College station, near dark. Hitch-Hiking was fairly common back then and we all did it at some time or the other, especially college kids and the armed force personnel. Later when I attended college at Lamar Tech in Beaumont, Texas, I often used my thumb to get back to Malakoff during holidays. Royce and I felt totally safe, and I guess we were. I am sure we wore our Malakoff letter jackets and Royce had a small Aggie labeled bag with him. Sometimes when hitching a ride, you had to take a chance, because you never knew what sort of driver you might get. Standing on the road in cold weather with rain, and car after car whizzing by you, made you realize if you wanted to get to your destination, you had to trust the Lord to send you a good ride. Prayer was a necessity and we used it often. I do not remember how many rides it required to get us to College Station, but we made it!! Again, the good Lord had taken care of us as we traveled. Another possible mess Royce had gotten me into. It was that Thursday night that I spent the night somewhere in Walton Hall and met some of Royce's Aggie teammates. I remember Royce introducing me to the group and shaking hands with several, but much is still hidden from my memory. After doing research of the varsity roster that year, several familiar names appear.

THIS WAS THE AGGIE VARSITY ROSTER FOR 1956.

Roddy Osborne, QB
Jimmy Wright, OB
John David Crow, RB
Loyd Taylor, RB
Jack Pardee, RB
Don Watson, RB
Bobby Joe Conrad, RB
George Gilar, RB
Carlos Esquivel, RB
Luther Hall, RB
Bobby Marks, WR
John Tracey, WR

Gene Stallings, WR
Bobby Drake Keith, WR
Don Smith, WR
Dennis Goehring, OL
Lloyd Hale, OL
Charlie Krueger, OL
Jack Powell, OL
Jim Stanley, OL
Bobby Lockett, OL
Carl Luna, OL
Dee Powell, OL

I have attempted to find the '56 Freshman roster but have been unable to do so. Since Royce left this Earth in the early 70's I can't ask him who I met, but what I do remember is one name I later crossed paths with. In late 60's I began teaching at Sam Houston High school and one of the football coaches was a former '56 Aggie Football player, Bobby Marks. Another Sam Houston teacher/coach was Carlos Esquivel. Whether he was the same as the one on the Aggie roster, I don't know. Other notable names include, John David Crow, the Heisman trophy winner, Jack Pardee, later coach of the Gamblers pro team and the University of Houston. Gene Stallings who coached A&M to a SWC title in 1967 and was later the coach at Alabama, Royce was teammates with some really outstanding people and there I was amongst them. We were together in some dining area, not sure where. I was Royce's guest and he had introduced me to the group. Royce was required, as were all the freshmen, to sit and eat in a certain fashion. It was done in a robotic fashion in which they had to intake their food in only a certain way. Each bite must be taken in a certain way. Each drink the same. It was reaching out and griping the utensil and then in a square-to-square fashion, placing it in one's mouth. I remember when they wanted milk they asked for "cows". If you remember the entire Aggie student body was military back, then and the Aggie Footballers were also military. However, they had their own set of rules and regulations. I think we may have been in Sbisa Hall. Blaring in the background was music I to this day can still almost hear, "Day-0h, Day-Oh, Day Light Come and I wanna go Home!!" These were words from "The Banana Boat Song". Royce had previously told me he would need to study Thursday night so he could pass his English test on Friday. I had agreed and understood, but it never happened. Instead, we headed for the local pool hall and proceeded to shoot pool into the early hours, perhaps now Friday. Royce did not pass his English exam and in fact, I'm not sure if he passed anything that semester. After Royce's exam, we thumbed it back home and as far as our return trip, I remember nothing. We arrived back in Malakoff without any major problems and when I returned to class the following Monday, I found out I had been elected student body president. This happened.... without even trying. I am still wondering how it happened and how I was able to make this trip. Thank the good Lord I did and made it home safely.

My Student Council Tenure

As I have previously said, one of the biggest surprises of my high school career was my election as student body president. The articles in both the school paper "The Tiger Rag" and the Malakoff News Headlined:

MALAKOFF HIGH SCHOOL

ELECTS FIRST STUDENT COUNCIL

It didn't take long for a letter to the editor of the Malakoff News quickly contradicting this. In 1942, Raymond Reese was elected president of Malakoff's first student council.

We all knew Raymond because he was married to Kirby's daughter and was a well-known member of Kirby's grocery store staff. After Kirby's closed, he worked at Brookshire Brothers.

I don't suppose at the time it really mattered because I was indeed the council president and boy did, I have a lot to learn. We had an activity period for all students, which came before noon every day, and this was when the student council was to meet. Bob Farmer was our sponsor, another cap they had given him to wear. Mr. Farmer could now add to his swelling duties: assistant football coach, head boys' basketball, head girls' basketball, bus driver, history teacher, chemistry teacher and who knows what else. Oh, yes, he was the senior sponsor, which meant he was helping with our senior play as well as going on our senior trip. How did he do it? I don't think we met for student council every day, or at least I didn't. Not only was I among the "first" presidents elected, in all likely hood, I was one of the "worst". It was my student body officers who carried the load and really did all of the work, because I was more interested in playing during activity period. So, instead of going to council meetings, I went to play basketball in the gym. Without Judy Farmer and Henry Allen, I doubt anything would have been accomplished. My other officers: Delores McLain, Judy Farmer, Glenn Conditt, Ellen Rogers, Deanna Poole, Jerry Andrews, Henry Allen, Tommy Wallace were the real student council. I remember being given the duty of announcing at our Girls' basketball tournament. As a "supposed to be" announcer I was so nervous my knees were knocking and perhaps wet in some improper places. Thanks to my good friend, Henry (Mitch) Allen, I was saved. He was at the mike with me and did all of the announcing, with me being strictly a figure head. Since Mitch had experience with singing in his band, he was a great choice. So, Henry had rescued me from total failure.

Another thing the student council tried was a plea directed to the alums asking them to donate money. We obtained a list of Alums and sent them all a postcard (they were priced at a whole 1 cent), requesting a donation to establish a fund used to build tennis courts. To my knowledge we received exactly **zero** replies.

Malakoff high school never had a prom before, at least none we knew of and some of us began talking about having one. I think we got our idea when some of us were in attendance of a dance at the National Guard Armory in Athens one Saturday. From this Amory dance, the idea of a junior/senior prom began to be explored. So, with the foresight of a real president, I called for a student council meeting and began to set up committees in charge of certain things. Suddenly, I morphed into a person completely presidential. The evolution and timing were perfect. I set up committees for: securing the Amory, finding a band, refreshments, rules for the dance and numerous other committees. It went so well in our meeting; it was as if I were another person. My out of body experience was destined to quickly end. The bell rang to end activity period and as I was headed back to class the loud speaker came on. You remember those little boxes in all of the rooms where the announcements were made, well I clearly heard, "Don Henderson, please report to Mr. Starkey's office." Suddenly a lump jumped in my throat, and I knew I was in big trouble. Mr. Starkey was our Superintendent/Principal and a staunch Baptist as well. I never got into trouble, so for me to be called into his office meant trouble. By trying to set up this dance, it went against not only the Baptist Church, but my own as well because dancing was not an option and was a sin. As my heart raced and the sound pounded in my freighted ears, I nervously walked to the office to take my medicine. Mr. Starkey said immediately, "You know why you are here, don't you?" "Yes, sir," I uttered. "You know you cannot have a school dance, for several reasons." "First of all, it is against school board rules, and besides you are holding it off campus, which is against the rules." "You will not have a prom, understood." As I cowed, I sheepishly replied, "Yes, sir." So, the first, sorry, second, student body president who finally had become presidential had the wind knocked completely out his sails and there would be no prom. I soon learned the reason I was so quickly called in. It was because one of my committee members as they went back to class stopped by and invited Mr. Starkey to the dance. From there it all went downhill.

Golden Gloves 1957

Below is evidence to substantiate that I did enter the Golden Gloves competition in Tyler, Feb 4-5-6-7-9, 1957. Note: Most all "hung up their gloves" well before the 9th.

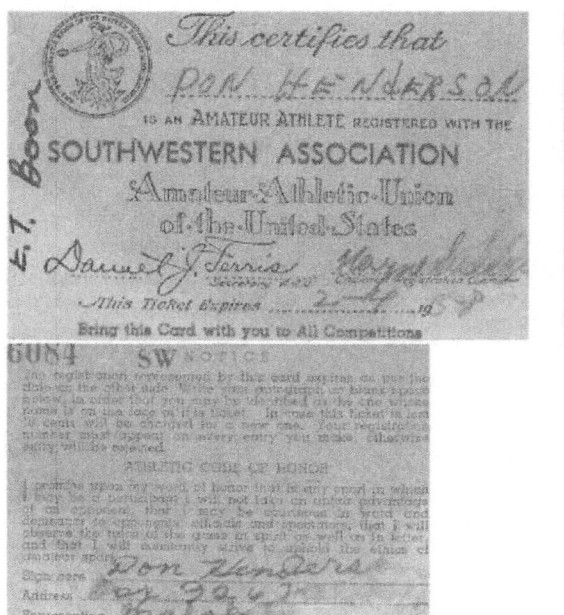
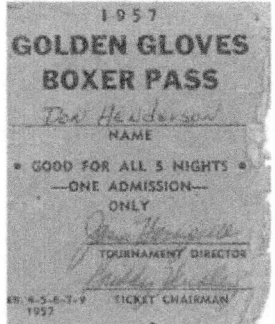

Sign-in/weigh-in took place at Tyler Junior college, there I had to join the Southwestern Association, Amateur Athletic Union of the United States and I signed the ATHLETIC CODE OF HONOR, which read:

I promise upon my word of honor that in any sport in which I may be a participant I will not take an unfair advantage of an opponent, that I may be courteous in word and demeanor to opponents, officials and spectators, that I will observe the rules of the game in spirit as well as in letter, and that I will constantly strive to uphold the ethics of amateur sport.

WHO ENTERED GOLDEN GLOVE COMPETITION?

Note: In the **January 30** issue, Athens Review,1957 Bill Speake reported: Entered in the East Texas Golden Gloves competition from Henderson County are: Don Henderson, Buster Carter, Earl Ray Andrews, Milburn Holt, James Cope, Ken Andrews, Royce Shelton, Sonny Humphries, Herman Rogers, Mack Hatton, Jerry Kemp, John Bates, Elgie Owen, Richard Jackson, C.L. Gideon, Harold Owen, R.E. Saxon, Kelly Whitehead, Hamilton Leach, James Colley, Loyd Nichols, Bob Massey, Travis Craig, Don Kennedy.

**Gary Spivey was listed as being on the card, but not listed as an original entry. I do not remember Gary boxing, although I do remember him being one of my good teammates on the Tiger football team where he played fullback. Not sure why my name came first.

Note: In the **February 11, 1957,** Athens Review, Bill Speake, in his column: "Speaking of Sports", reported the following: There were 26 boys from Henderson County. There were 12 from Brownsboro, 10 from Malakoff, and 4 from Athens entered in this year's East Texas Golden Gloves competition.

It was another fine mess Royce got us into. Sometime in the 2nd semester of my senior year, Royce began to "round-up" Malakoff potential boxers. The only Southside members Royce coerced were Eddie and I, but Eddie later declined to enter.... I should have. We began having some practice rounds in the Shelton's front yard. Royce had some extra gloves and he matched me up with Earl Ray Andrews. We exchanged a few licks and then Sonny "Fingers" Humphries and I went a few rounds. The only previous time I ever had gloves on was during a summer visit with my Mother in Pt. Neches, when one of the neighborhood kids (younger than I) was a boxer. Royce encouraged us to enter the competition in Tyler and he talked Alton Allen into being our coach/driver. Previously Royce had not only done some boxing, but he also was familiar with a bit of street fighting. None of the rest of us had ever been in a ring and I was never one to engage in fist-a-cuffs. The only way that I felt comfortable hitting someone was on the football field; where I could freely knock the snot out of someone and not have a guilty conscience. A short time before we had completed our 1956 football season and I was in excellent condition, or at least thought I was. Royce said all you have to do is go three rounds for three minutes each round. Royce said, "You can do that!!" I thought to myself, three minutes, anyone can last that long. Royce recruited Buster Carter, Sonny Humphries, Hoss Cope, Milburn Holt, me, Earl Ray Andrews, and Ken Andrews. In addition, someway, Herman Rogers was recruited. Herman (actually my Uncle, but too close to my age to call him Uncle) had just come back from a stint in the army and was a true street fighter, so Royce figured he would be good in the ring. Royce was home from his short stay as a Texas A&M footballer, but due to a broken hand injury and academics, his time at A&M was over. By this time his hand had completely healed, and he was in excellent condition, so he thought he had a good chance in the ring. I guess you could call Royce our "promoter" and organizer. So, with this contingency we were off to Tyler to battle in our first Golden Gloves bouts, not knowing that for the majority of us it would be our last. We all had to report for weigh-in so we could enter a weight class. I weighed-in at a strapping 118 lbs. of solid muscle and mighty bones. They said I was a "feather weight" (although in the paper it reported that I was Bantam weight) and this meant that I would be fighting against people my own size, unlike football in which everyone out-weighed me. I still remember a guy from Forney named Mahondro who played tackle at the "light" weight of 230 lbs. It was my job to block this behemoth, which I could do if I hit him at his ankles and then prepare myself for the mountain to fall on me. Somehow, I was never hurt. (Thanking the Lord again).

In the weight in room, I was able observe several of the ring contestants as they warmed up. The one boxer who caught my attention was the kid who was punching one of those long bags that are about three or four foot long, suspended by a rope. This guy was punching that bag and hitting it again and again, turning the bag parallel to the floor at a 90-degree angle. He was good!! I wondered who he was and overheard a conversation in which someone said, "That's E.T. Boone, last year's state champion in his weight class." Having never entered a boxing tournament before, I was understandably nervous, but seeing this dude, made me even more nervous. Our next step was to see when we boxed and I was surprised to learn that I had drawn a first-round bye, I was excited because this basically meant that I had won my first round and would not be boxing until Wednesday night. My excitement quickly dissipated when I learned my first opponent was E.T. Boone!! Of all the ones recruited by Royce, he couldn't get Eddie to agree to box. He was the smart one. Memory escapes me as to who road in Alton Allen's car, but I do remember some details. I believe Eddie went along with us; I suppose as "moral" support. Alton had graduated from Malakoff in 1948, so back then 9 years made him an old dude to us. Alton's car was a brand-new Cadillac and had all of the latest fancy features, including a floorboard button to change radio stations, which he played as we traveled. Our coach/manager was one of our heroes we looked up to and he was enjoying his position of helping us. Cannot remember for sure where we connected with Alton, whether he came and picked me up or I met him somewhere. I remember riding in the back seat of that big car and enjoying that 38-mile trip to Tyler from Malakoff. In a few hours, all would change. The first bouts were scheduled for February, February 5, 1957.Since I was scheduled to box the second night, I became an eyewitness to what I would describe as a "slaughter" the first night. As I set as a member of the audience, I watched each of our Malakoff boys go down, one by one. The scenes in my memory bank are not the correct sequence, but the parade of downed Malakoff fighters is inscribed indelibly in my mind. Earl Ray was one of the first of our group to meet his challenger. E. Ray danced around, throwing wild punches, while his opponent carefully eyed him. His opponent hardly moved, as he stood central with E. Ray circling him. This seemed to go on for an eternity, but not nearly as long as it does when you yourself are in the ring. If I were to guess, I would say, about two minutes had passed and Earl Ray's opponent had blocked Earl's jabs but had yet to swing any. So quick I barely saw it, and I am sure E. Ray didn't, all of a sudden E. Ray's opponent, Raymond Roark of Tyler, landed one mighty blow and Earl Ray literally went down like a toppled tree in 1:30 of the first round. He was down for the count.

Next up was Buster Carter. Buster had a different tactic because his opponent was engaged in trying to chase Buster down because Buster was doing his best imitation of a scared rabbit as he literally ran around the ring, hoping to avoid being hit. It wasn't long until Buster was lying flat of his back and the ref called a TKO in 1:38 of the opening round by Jimmy Parker of Grand Saline. Now there were two down. I began to plan for my bout, and I was determined that E.T. was Not going to knock me out. Up next was our street fighter, Herman, who I thought had a good chance to win. The two boxers exchanged blows at random and each got some pretty good licks in. At least Herman made it out of the 1st round without being KO-ed. Herman managed a 2nd round also, and his opponent was showing signs of Herman's Street fighting ability. Years of smoking and being out of shape finally caught up with Herman and he succumbed. Herman swung and missed, and his opponent landed a mighty blow and Herman went down in the second round. As I sat in the audience watching this, it appeared to me that Herman took the 10 count and the knockout just to be able to escape the ring. Three men up and three down. Sonny Humphries made a match of it against Glenn Hill of Arp but lost in a decision. These bouts I remember. As I watched my friends being taken out, I became even more determined that E.T. would not knock me out. Reflecting back on this "mess" that Royce had gotten us all into, I wondered why we let him convince us to enter, but we did. Speaking of E.T., as I write this, I find an ironic twist.... E.T. was later a movie about an Extra-Terrestrial, and perhaps he was. Trying to piece together my Golden Gloves story after some 60 years requires more than just my memory. It also required reading some of the articles that were written by Bill Speake, sportswriter for the Athens Review. Even with this, it has become a complicated task trying to put it all back together. There are vivid parts of my time in the ring which flash back to me in glorious detail. In fact, some of it flashes in my mind as if it happened yesterday. After reading Speake's account of my fight, I don't remember it exactly as he. The following is the way I remember my 1_{st} and last boxing match. I entered the ring Wednesday night, determined not to go down, but E.T. had other ideas. E.T. was the champ from the year before and not only was he experienced he was skilled. Before I ever entered the ring, I had witnessed his skills on the punching bag and now I was about to become one. Alton coached me before I entered the ring and encouraged me to just do my best. Before any of these bouts took place, I didn't know I would need to use a mouthpiece, but I now had one. I'm pretty sure someone else in our group had previous used it and "all precautions for cleanliness" were made. NOT! The first thing I remember came early in the first round. (I kept reminding myself, three minutes is nothing, easy to last three minutes). And then the first blow.... you've heard of hearing birdies when a boxer gets hit, well I now can confirm the truth. Not only did I hear birdies after the first lick, I saw double or maybe even triple. According to Bill Speake I was knocked down twice in the 2nd round, well I believe that is true, but what he didn't report is that I was knocked down three times in the first round and each time I got up, praying for the bell to sound. This was absolutely the longest three minutes ever. During either the 1st or 2nd round is when I spit out my mouthpiece and I can't remember why. By this time, I was standing only by my sheer determination. When round one ended and I went to my corner, or perhaps staggered, Alton gave me water and wet my forehead. My lip was busted, and I could feel that one eye was going to be black. According to Speake's column, I took a 9 count in the 2nd round, and I suppose that was true. If I had had any sense, I would have stayed down, but this dumb country boy got up and finished the round. I can still feel my hurts and my vision distortion which I was experiencing. I kept reminding myself, "Don't give up!!" I somehow managed to make it to the 3rd round by the grace of God, barely hanging on. I think E.T. was so tired from pounding on me that he was too tired to hit me hard enough to knock me out in the 3rd. His unanimous decision came as no surprise, but I had accomplished my goal of not being knocked out. That really was a "relative term" because I was literally out on my feet after the very first blow. Later I found out that match was being broadcast on the radio and my Grandfather Tom Rogers later told me that he had been listening. Granddad said, "Son, I thought you were getting killed from the way that announcer was broadcasting the bout!!" "I was Granddaddy!!" During the ride home I had a certain amount of pride that I had survived my licking and I was resigned to the fact that though I had not won, to me I had not lost. The next day at school, I proudly displayed my two black eyes, my busted lip, and my intact pride. It was then, I reminded myself, Don, never, ever, enter Golden Gloves again, so now 60 years later I'm glad I had that one bout and even happier that I never had another.

The following poem or song was written by an unknown Malakoff Student. I suspect it was someone in our '57 Journalism class. I asked Kenneth Carrol if the writing was his, but he declared it was not. The way it is written, I think it might have been Ronnie Stockman. Since he passed away before I found this copy, I cannot ask him. Whoever the author was it was written about our

Malakoff losing boxing contingency. Those who will remember spirit duplicators, the original was typed and run off on a spirit duplicator, which is the long-ago old way of doing things, long before printers and computers. It was **titled** "Banana Boat Song", which I assume was copied after a then popular song by the same title.

Banana Boat Song

By Unknown Malakoff High Student from 1957

1. Buster Carter went to Tyler, to fight in the ring
3:25 and I want to go home.
He soon heard nothing but hear birdies sing.
3:25 and I want to go home.
Buster, Buster, 3:25 and I want to go home.

2. Pedro Henderson marched in like a Jellybean.
3:25 and I want to go home.
He wished a little later He's never been seen.
3:25 Pedro, Pedro

3. Another Tyler fighter was Ole Hoss Cope,
3:25 and I want to go home.
But he couldn't cope with the boy in the rope,
3:25 and I want to home James, James,
3:25 and I want to go home.

4. Sonny Humphries said watch that boy is slow,
3:25, and I want to home.
But soon Old Sonny couldn't even go,
3:25 and I want to go home Sonny, Sonny,
3:25 and I want to go home.

5. Our mamas and papas come up in a stew,
3:25 and I want to go home.
What they don't know is their kids IQ,
3:25 and I want to go home Mamas, Papas,
3:25 and I want to go home.

6. Well I sleep at school, and I ramble at night,
3:25 and I want to go home.
Most of time my conduct is not right,
3:25 and I want to go home Poor me, Poor me,
3:25 and I want to go home.

7. The teachers they say are wanting more mon,
3:25 and I want to go home.
But it doesn't matter; they are teaching for fun,
3:25 and I want to go home Teachers, Teachers,

8. Mr. Starkey doesn't like the hot rod car,
3:25 and I want to go home.
You'd better be careful he can see you far,
3:25 and I want to go home Starkey, Starkey

9. Coach Loggins he says don't chew that gum,
3:25 and I want to go home.
I suggest to you, just bring him some,
3:25 and I want to go home.
Loggins, Loggins

10. Mr. Farmer in chemistry wants you to spell,
3:25 and I want to go home.
But what I don't like is that awful smell,
3:25 and I want to go home Farmer, Farmer

11. Well, I'm griping about my school grades, all day long,
3:25 and I want to go home.
Every one of these teachers are grading me wrong,
3:25 and I want to go home.
Griping, Griping,

12. I am sure you've liked this brand-new song,

3:25 and I want to go home.

Give me a quarter and we'll send you along,

3:25 and I want to go home.

Bill Speake: Speaking of Sports, Feb 5, 1957, Tuesday, after our Monday night fights. Selected Text from Athens Review.

Kenneth Andrews of Malakoff, Kelly Whitehead of Athens, R.E. Saxon, James Colley, Mack Hatton and Richard Jackson all from Brownsboro were victorious in first round action.

Andrews whipped Kenneth Voyles of Lindale in one of the liveliest fights of the evening. The Malakoff youth dropped his opponent for an eight count in the third and hammered him all over the ring the rest of the round. By the time it ended Voyles was barely on his feet. Hatton took a unanimous decision in a bout with Don Bird of Garrison. In the opening fight on the card, Jackson won his fight the easy way...by default. His opponent, Larry Camper of Van, failed to appear.

Whitehead pounded out a decision over Larry Dike of Tyler and Saxon knocked out O.C. Parr of New London. Colley won over his opponent by default.

John Bates of Athens and Johnny Carlisle of New London on pretty equal terms with Carlisle taking a split decision.

Elgie Owen of Brownsboro was TKO'd in 25 seconds of the second round in his battle with Don Pierce.

Don Bass of Van won by a TKO over Jerry Kemp of Athens in 39 seconds of the first round.

Milburn Holt lost to Dean Rhinehart of Arp by a unanimous decision. (I do not remember Milburn boxing, but I do remember him as a good football team member)

Loyd Nichols of Brownsboro started strong but lost to Dwain Walton of Tyler. After winning the first round, Nichols was knocked out or driven out of the ring in the second. Walton took command and won the match.

Bouts tonight, Tuesday, Feb. 5, 1957, include Doyle Barnard of Hallsville vs. Hamilton Leach of Brownsboro, Richard Jackson of Brownsboro vs. Bob Kennedy of Lindale, Tom McGuire of Arp vs. Harold Owens of Brownsboro, Billy Hopkins of Van vs. James Colley of Brownsboro. Jack Henry of Tyler vs. Bobby Massey of Brownsboro, Kelly Whitehead vs. of Athens vs. R.E. Saxon of Brownsboro, James Henry of Tyler vs. Gary Spivey of Malakoff, David Evans of Athens vs. Gene Gallien of Hallsville, Travis Craig of Brownsboro vs. James Cope of Malakoff, Eugene Bates of Grand Saline vs. Royce Shelton of Malakoff, and Leo Barbary of Longview vs. Don Kennedy of Brownsboro.

Some 25 fights will be held tonight, beginning at 7:30 p.m. Almost 1,800 fans attended Monday night.

Colley, Evans, Kennedy, Face Tough Test In Semi-Finals At Tyler Today, Thursday, Feb 7, 1957

FEB 7, 1957, TYLER, Texas — James Colley of Brownsboro, David Evans of Athens, **Royce Shelton** of Malakoff, and Don Kennedy of Brownsboro are the only Henderson County fighters still in contention in the East Texas Golden Gloves Tournament.

As these boys prepare for the semi-finals tonight, some 22 others who represented Henderson County are hanging up their gloves, at least for another year.

Colley, a 133 pounder, will battle Ronnie Walker, 135, of Hallsville. Evans, 152, will take on Douglas Bruner, 157, of Longview. Shelton, 172, battles Pete Burks, 175, of. Longview, and Kennedy, 167, takes on Bob Franks, 174, of Tyler.

Wednesday night, Colley decisioned Tom McGuire, 135, of Arp, Evans scored a TKO over Buddy Cochran, 154, of Longview in the second round, Shelton TKO'd Weldon Hardin, 165, of Longview, second round, and Kennedy won by a second round TKO over Pat Parish, 166, of Longview... Henderson County's only open division fighter — **Herman Rogers** of Malakoff, a middleweight —was KO'd by Donnie Odom of Carthage. The end came in the second round after the two fighters had battled on even terms throughout the first. **Rogers** threw a punch and

missed and was nailed with a solid right hook that put him down for the count. Jerry Hatton of Brownsboro, a flyweight, was TKO'd by Larry Page of Hallsville in 1:30 of the opening round. **Don Henderson** was decisioned by E. T. Boone of Tyler. **Henderson** was down in the second round and took a nine-count.

C. L. Gideon of Brownsboro, a welterweight, was decisioned by Bill Wadington of Arp, and R. E. Saxon lost by a decision to Tony Roberts of Arp.

James Cope of Malakoff suffered a first-round knockout at the hands of Harpie Pettiet of Grand Saline in a middleweight bout.

About 24 fights are scheduled for tonight in the Gentry Gym ring.
Above is Bill Speake's description of my beating, dated Feb 7, 1957.

Royce made it at least to the semi-finals before he was beaten. I will always believe he laid down. The reason: I think he may have entered as a Novice and he had other bouts which would have changed his eligibility. I could not find anything about Kenneth Andrews' later bouts, but perhaps the same thing happened to him. My Golden Gloves experience was one that I shall never forget. Royce, should I thank you for another fine mess you got me into …or………….???

After The '55 Team, Nokes No Joke

By Don Henderson

It was in the summer of '56 when our football team began our practices. Gone were the dynamic seniors of the '56 graduating class. Royce Shelton was off to Texas A&M and Coach Bear Bryant. Royce was an outstanding back for the Tigers and who could replace him? Donald Jordan was now playing for Rice University and Coach Jess Neely. Donald was our quarterback/running back in Coach Loggins 1955 offense. Both Royce and Donald were All-County and were basically irreplaceable. Dickie Derden, who played end, was another outstanding player, as well as linesman, Johnny Mack Brown, Bobby Rogers, Stanley (Red) Johnson and Howard Hardy. In addition, Ken Andrews, another all-district player would be leaving us because of age limit. Ben Garcia, another All-District player, was also 19 and would not return for our '56 football season. It was said the '55 backfield, consisting of Royce Shelton, Don Jordan, Ken Andrews and Neil Williams (then a sophomore) was the fastest in Henderson County, perhaps in the state. Royce was a 10 flat hundred man and Don and Ken were nearly as fast. Neil was under 12, which was considered fast in '55. So, 9 of our starters from 1955 season would not return. No wonder Coach Loggins, when asked by the Athens Review what he thought about the Malakoff Football upcoming season, he replied: "I'll sure be glad when basketball season gets here!!" Who could blame him? Our first game of the season was with our old rival, Mabank and as expected we were big underdogs. Our '55 team had demolished Mabank 49-0 the last game of the '55 season, so Mabank was very fired up and intent on beating Malakoff. On the other hand, our '56 Tiger team was determined not to let it happen. We knew our chances were not good, but we were not deterred by all of the predictions. Mabank probably thought they were going to run all over us. The three senior returning lettermen on the '56 team were me, Eddie Nokes and Bo Johnson. The rest of the team consisted of mostly inexperienced juniors, sophomores and the new freshmen. A great addition was senior, Kenneth Carter. Kenneth, who was a very good basketball player, was persuaded to join the team. Kenneth had never played football before, but being a big tough country boy from Crossroads, we figured he might fool some people....and he did. Bo and I were listed at 125, but neither weighed that even soaking wet. Perhaps coach listed us that way because he didn't want to be embarrassed by our real weight. The setting was made for a Malakoff Massacre by Mabank. In the 60 years which passed, I had searched for the Athens Review sports article entitled: **"Nokes No Joke"**, but having looked through all my clippings numerous times, I never found it. I gave up and wrote the article as best I could, but after 60 years, memories fade. It was not until the original Bill Speake article was located when all the true facts came to light. Thanks to my good friend Ken Carrol found his copy of the article and sent it to me. It was such a thrill to finally have that article. I had previously written my own version for my good buddy and Southside member, Eddie Nokes. The story was posted on Facebook in celebration of Eddie's August birthday. It was not until later I found the real story, which appears after my version.

MY RENDITION OF "Nokes No Joke" When we were seniors and our football team had lost Royce and Donald and all of those good players from the 1956 team. Eddie, Bo and I were the only ones left from all of the others that would have been in our class. (In elementary school we had some big boys who would have grown even larger. (Bobrow Gunnels, Jax Baird, Fred Jenkins and several more) Kenneth Carter was drafted to play, but he had to learn a new rule every time the lined up because they didn't play football in Crossroads. The fire which destroyed Crossroads School during the summer of '53 brought Malakoff several good athletes and we were especially lucky to get Kenneth who was an outstanding basketball player.

The Athens sports reporter (Bill Speake) interviewed Coach Loggins, asking what he thought about the upcoming football season. When his answer hit the news the following morning, we all saw his answer, "I'll sure be glad when basketball season gets here!!" Now reflecting back, after doing some coaching in high school myself, I can understand his answer, but at the time our team was furious. Hoss Cope talked us into a cute scenario which proved to get us in big trouble with Coach Loggins. Hoss suggested every time we got a chance we should "dribble" the football. So, that day as we lined up to run out for passes, we would grab the football with one hand and dribble it. Coach Loggins and Coach Farmer soon took the wind out of our sails when we had to run wind sprints for about 30 minutes. This was August and it was "HOT!!" No drinking water, only a sip, was the absolute law then. We soon got the point!! No more dribbles. That week we had our first game of the season scheduled and Mabank was a heavy favorite. We were determined to beat Mabank and prove Coach wrong. Coach Loggins and Coach Farmer devised a plan with Eddie at fullback and Bo Johnson at halfback. The day after the game the headlines in the Athens paper read, **"NOKES NO JOKE!!"** That night Eddie scored a touchdown, threw a touchdown pass to Bo, and kicked about a 50-yard quick kick. He destroyed Mabank with outstanding rushing yardage. We won **13-12** and it was a miracle. Eddie did play fullback in several more games, but I suppose Coach saw Eddie's weight of 175 running behind me a hefty 125(stretching it) was not going to get it, so he switched Eddie back to tackle. We finished the season 4-6 and by today's standards we would have placed 3rd. Good enough for a playoff spot.

NOKES NO JOKE

The following are excerpts from Bill Speake's original 1956 article.

TO BE PERFECTLY honest, Malakoff's big Eddie Nokes was the difference between victory and sure defeat for Coach Bill Loggins' charges Friday night. I have seen many backs as good or better in the running department, but I have never seen a converted lineman step into the backfield and become the number one ball totter from the outset. Nokes played fullback as if he has been there for years instead of for just a few days of practice. As a tackle, Nokes also excelled, winning all district honors twice. He weighs 175pounds and is a senior. In Friday night's game, Nokes was a terror ripping huge chunks of yardage off almost every time he lugged the ball. He ripped the Mabank line to shreds on several occasions. Not that he manhandled Mabank's front wall; he also was smeared several times. With Nokes moving the ball, Malakoff might stand a better chance in District 18-A than a lot of people think, but don't expect the Tigers to finish first. Canton seems a shoo-in in the preseason ratings. But then so did Rice in 1955.

More by Bill Speake

GOOD DEFENDERS

THERE WERE several top hand defensive players on both teams. One of these was Kenneth Carter, who made all Henderson County in basketball last season. Carter never played football until this season, but he was one of the most impressive wranglers on the field, tearing into the Mabank backs as though he had a personal grudge to settle with all and sundry. A spectator at the game told me Carter's father didn't want him to play football because he felt the game was too rough. I'll bet there are some Mabank boys who didn't know how rough it was until they met up with Kenneth. What Carter did to Mabank was paid back in full by the Panthers' all-district lineman Alton Frosch. He stayed on those Malakoff backs so closely that they must have thought he belonged there. Speaking of linemen, Eddie Nokes should certainly give big Paul Bankston a pat on the back. He opened those gaping holes and gave Nokes running room on the right side.

I was thrilled to finally, after some 60 years, to be able to read the real "Nokes No Joke" article. Bill Speake lauded over my good buddy, Eddie, but he was not the only Southside member who was a hero that night. In addition to Eddie, Paul Davis (P.D.) Bankston was mentioned for his opening up holes on the right side for Eddie. I too was on that right side, hurling my heavy (125 lbs.) frame into those Mabank boys, while P.D. destroyed them with his massive 200 lbs. + frame. We were quick to award Kenneth Carter an honorary Southside membership because Crossroads was after all on the Southside of Malakoff. What a thrill to remember this 13-12 win, which was indeed a miracle.

Royce and Golf

Back in the late 60's when John Farrell and I lived together in Houston we talked Royce into joining us for a golf game. It was always my desire growing up to beat Royce at something.... well; I could do that with Golf. As bad as I was, Royce was worse. Of course, John could shoot in the 70's back then and me in the 90-100's. We played at Glenbrook golf course over on the East side of Houston. As the day moved along it became obvious Royce could not hit a golf ball out of his own shadow. There were two guys in front of us who John and I had to wait for, but we worried little about Royce's shots. After 17 holes of hitting the ball an incredible 75 yards with his driver, Royce was still a good sport about it. Upon occasion, when we went with Royce to a bar, a threat of a fight often had ensued. Royce always wore the muscle-men shirts to show off his biceps and most fights never happened after they looked at Royce's physique. We quickly learned not to go into bars with Royce. On this day, as we approached the 18th green, we reflected on how much fun we'd had. Over 200 yards away were the 2 guys ahead of us on the green. Of course, we said go ahead, Royce. Royce hit a ball that looked like a pro had hit it. It sailed about 30 ft. above the ground and rose to 50, dropping solidly into the back of one of the guys putting on 18. Without hesitation, the guy turned, swearing toward us. On his face was that look to kill. As he started back toward us; Royce, with his usual calm look, responded with his customary "bar" demeanor and stepped forward to meet his would-be assailant. The guy took one look at Royce, immediately calmed himself and very politely said, "It's Ok, no harm done!!" You know that blow to his back had to have hurt. If you have ever been hit with a golf ball, you know for several days, maybe even weeks the man's back was going to be sore.

Once again, John and I avoided a confrontation Royce started and which we had no part of but were about to be in the midst of. Needless to say, after these 18 holes with Royce Shelton, the next time we were certain the people ahead were off the green before we urged Royce to hit.

Clouds and Temptations

I suppose back in the 40's and 50's without TV, cell phone, the internet or any of today's devices, we had to be creative in order to entertain ourselves. I remember lying on our backs in Robertson's field, watching those puffy white clouds. As we lay there watching them, they would change. Eddie would explain, "There's a dog!" "Oh yea, I see it." Then I would say, no, "It's a dragon!!" and it was, the cloud had just changed. We could lay there for a long time, watching changing, much like a kaleidoscope. The same game was played by my sister and I as we road along in the back seat of our parents' car. Much pleasure was derived from this simple exercise.

EDDIE'S TEMPTATION

During the 1950's my Granddad had an entire peach orchard in our backyard, next to the Nokes. A crop of some really big luscious peaches soon developed. These were the big Alberta peaches and when ripe they were delicious. There was one tree so near to the Nokes property it was within easy reaching distance. Eddie observed the daily development of this tempting fruit and longed for a taste, so one day he reached over and snagged that peach. I never knew about it at the time because neither Eddie nor my Granddad ever said anything. Years later, after my

Granddad had passed away, Eddie confessed to me and commented about how good that peach was. He said, "I'm pretty sure Mr. Henderson knew I took it, but he never said anything." "I think I know why." I told Eddie. "For one, we had plenty of them, but the other reason may have had to do with his boyhood experience with apples." When he was a young boy in Mississippi his Dad gave him strict instructions not to pick any of the apples because he wanted to see how big they would get. So, my Granddad obeyed. He ate the apples and left the core and stem hanging on the tree.

Eddie's New Rod and Reel

After graduating from high school, Eddie found a job somewhere and became a cherished credit card holder. His brand-new credit was with Sears and Roebuck (known as Sears now). As soon as I heard of his new acquisition, I knew what my good buddy would buy. It would be something to do with fishing or hunting and I was right. He bought a brand-new rod and reel, one of those fancy kinds with a star drag on it, which could even be used in salt water, even though we were miles from the coast. Royce suggested we go fishing at the old cut-off, which was a branch of the Trinity, long cut off from the main tributary, but known to have a plentiful supply of fish. We had fished here before and knew lurking in those waters were good sized catfish, bass, and a plentiful supply of perch and perhaps even an elusive gar. In the past we had hooked gar but had never caught one because they always escaped after being hooked. We each had a rod and reel as well as some plain ole bamboo fishing poles and a few minnows and earthworms for bait. We were ready to catch something interesting, maybe even enough for a good meal. So, we baited our hooks and began fishing. The bamboo poles allowed us to fish for the shallower fish, so we used corks. The idea was to have as many hooks in the water as we could get, hoping for a good strike. Royce and I were using our rod and reel with lures and casting here and there, hoping to get a bite. Meanwhile, Eddie decided to bait his brand-new rig with a perch he had previously caught. He cast his line out and let his heavy sinker carry it to the bottom, then set the rod on the bank with the "star" on. Eddie then went about the business of checking the bamboo lines for a possible nibble. He spotted one cork bobbing up and down and so he went to check it. Often turtles would be the nibbler and Eddie figured this was a turtle, but you never know, so he grabbed the pole and waited for the cork to go under. We each had a bamboo pole, put it was a joint project and we all three watched for the bobbing of either of the baited poles. While Eddie was engaged with this nibble, Royce and I continued our casting and occasionally we would get a slight strike, but so far, we had not caught anything.

All of a sudden, we heard a sound, and we knew it was the line of Eddie's brand-new rig being taken out. As soon as Eddie heard it, he quickly forgot about the cane pole nibble and headed toward where his rod and reel lay. He was perhaps 50 yards away when he first heard it and was casual, even ambling toward his rig, but all of a sudden he realized something big must be on the line, so he ran as fast as he could, arriving just in time to see his brand new rod and reel being taken into the waters. He dived for it, but it was too late, it was gone!! Eddie stood on the banks flabbergasted and wondering what creature now had his brand-new rig. I think this pretty well ended our fishing for the day, at least for Eddie. It wasn't until later; he realized he was going to get a Sears Roebuck bill for a rod and reel, which he no longer possessed.

Grappling by Grandpa

Great Grandpa Roberts liked to fish in an unusual way according to my Granddad Oscar. Cedar Creek was in close proximity to Grandpa's land south of Malakoff. This was long before Cedar Creek Lake was built, which took away the original Cedar Creek. Cedar Creek was just another tributary of the Trinity River and was a place known for big catfish. One story related to me by my Grandmother Grace, tells of a wagon going by the Robert's place with a catfish as long as the bed of that wagon; a fish story indeed. This fish, if it did exist, was more than likely caught on a trotline; not the way Grandpa fished. My Granddad Oscar said he went with Grandpa on one of his fishing trips and as it turned out it was his first and last. As told by Granddad Oscar, Grandpa entered the water along the bank and Grandad followed. Grandpa began to move along the bank, reaching his hand into holes where fish might be hiding. This method called grappling was apparently frequently used by old timers. Grandpa had previously brought home a good mess of catfish using his method of grappling for fish, so Granddad went with him hoping to learn and copy his technique. Grandpa grabbed up and pulled out a couple of nice size three- or four-pound catfish and had them on a stringer. Grandad stayed near to observe and learn. This is when Grandpa reached in a grabbed another one, but this one he quickly threw backward, and it splashed beside Granddad. Only thing was it was a three- or four-foot water moccasin, which quickly slithered off.... along with Granddad. My

Granddad Oscar said when he saw that snake in the air, tossed by Grandpa; he sprouted wings and came up out of the water so fast he may have left skid marks. Now his pants were wet not only from the creek water, but also.... Without missing a beat, Grandpa, went right back to grappling, undisturbed by that snake, but Grandad stood rigid on the bank, wet pants and all, declaring never again to grapple fish with Grandpa.

Another way Grandpa fished was using a toe sack full of crushed black walnut sepals. The chemical exuded from the shells acted to cause the fish to roll to the surface seeking oxygen and then Grandpa would gather a mess of fish. Apparently, the chemical was like Rotenone used to get rid of trash fish when restocking a pond.

Raising Rabbits

I think my first pet rabbit experience came when I was about three years old living with my grandparents in Megargel, Texas. Someone gave me a baby cottontail small enough to fit into a regular sized kitchen matchbox. The rabbit in time grew and had free roam of our house. One night it grabbed its empty bowl with its teeth and began banging it on the floor, telling everyone that it wanted to be fed. This happened in my Aunt Martha's room, and it woke her. The rabbit had made its point. One night that rabbit ran across her face while she slept. Then one day my rabbit disappeared. Years later my grandmother confessed. She left the door open and allowed it to escape.

When I was about eight years old my rabbit tutorage was supplied by my Stepfather, Paul Powers. As were many of his schemes, he thought raising rabbits would lead to a profit, so in his Pt. Neches backyard he began raising rabbits. Beginning in about 1946, I became a summer visitor in Pt. Neches where my Stepfather, Mother and sister lived. In the backyard a rabbit cage housed a couple of white rabbits. At the time I can truthfully say I still thought storks brought babies, so maybe I was naïve enough to believe they brought rabbits.... surely not. Anyway, it wasn't long before the babies arrived and soon Paul (my stepfather) had a family of rabbits. Baby rabbits are cute little creatures and grow fast, so fast in fact it is not long before they are ready to have babies of their own. This I learned later. I also learned rabbits fight each other, or at least I thought it was fighting, but later concluded they were making love.... And more babies. Paul had no experience with rabbits, and I guess decided like chickens, you could ring their necks. You can't, and Paul quickly found this out because instead of ringing the poor rabbit's neck, he ended up choking the poor thing and it squealed and squealed before finally being clubbed with a hammer to get it out of its misery. He dressed the rabbit and readied it for Mother to cook. When the meal was served, every time I tried to take a bite, I could hear that poor rabbit squealing. Several years later with knowledge from my summer experience with rabbits in Pt. Neches, I decided to start my own rabbit farm in Malakoff. About the same time, Mr. Nokes, Eddie's dad (next door neighbors) began raising rabbits. My Granddad, Oscar helped me build a cage and a pair of rabbits was obtained from Mr. Nokes, so I was in business.... sort of. Not only are rabbits quick at love making, they also multiple quickly. Two become four, four become six, and etc., until soon you have a gaggle (not sure what you call a bunch of rabbits). I benefited from what I had witnessed with my Stepfather, and so did the rabbits. Rabbit meat is much like chicken, but all dark meat, which I learned from killing and eating cottontails. When they are your pets, the thought of killing one soon brings an end to wanting them for food. As my family of rabbits grew, so did my knowledge, not only of rabbits, but life processes as well. Some of my ideas about storks began to evolve. We had acquired a cage made of wire and with a roof. The cage was tall enough for me to stand up in. By this time, I had learned enough to know a female rabbit will be ready to mate at a fairly young age and the male rabbit also matures early. Often one of the male rabbits, which were kept in the tall cage, would be taken out and placed in a cage with a female ready to mate. Not long after we had little bunnies. One thing I never understood, the young female would actually eat her young sometime. This you needed to watch for.

One morning just before school, I was out tending to the rabbits. Eddie and I were talking across our back fence when I decided to put the buck rabbit back in the tall cage with the other bucks. Almost immediately after I placed the rabbit in the tall cage, a rabbit fight commenced, and fur was flying everywhere. Those rabbits were jumping in the air like two cats fighting. I immediately stepped into the cage to stop the fight and when I did, the rabbit which had just been placed in jumped toward my face about 4 or 5 feet into the air. I shielded my face as quickly as I could with my right arm, but as I did the rabbit bit me on my wrist, leaving a nasty bleeding cut. To this day, I still have a $1\ ^1/_2$ scar from that rabbit's bite. I tell people this story, and they don't believe it, but Eddie was an eyewitness and can vouch that it was true. By the grace of God, the bite missed any major blood vessels, but I was bleeding profusely and it was now time to go to school. Back then no one went to the doctor, and I most certainly was not going to tell my Grandmother, or she would have had a hissy fit. So, what did I do? I grabbed the old stand-by.... coal oil. Coal Oil was used for a lot of things, though probably never for a rabbit bite. After the coal oil was poured on, I wrapped it with a clean white cloth and went to school.

After a while, I think I grew tired of rabbits, especially cleaning out the poop in the cages, so Mr. Nokes told me the Smothers would take them. The Smothers were the owners and operators of St. Paul Industrial School, just northwest of downtown Malakoff and a few miles northeast of my Grandpa Robert's place. St. Paul was a home for orphan Black children. The orphans were the ones who worked Smother's farm. Mr. Nokes helped me load up those rabbits, cages and all, and he drove us to the Smother's farm where they gladly gave the rabbits a good home.

I thought I was out of the rabbit business, but I wasn't, not completely. Several years later, married and with our first child, one Easter, my stepdad brought my young son a rabbit. Of course, we couldn't turn it down because my son just loved it and so here, I was an un-proud owner of a white rabbit, back in the rabbit business again. Thanks a lot, Paul.

Easter Chickens

It was during Easter and my Grandmother, and I went to visit her cousin Bessie Cottle in Cleburne, Texas. I cannot remember if we took the bus or the train. We definitely did not go in a car because we didn't have one. The only thing I really remember about the trip was a stop we made on the way home and the little green baby chick I saw and had to have. It was a chick dyed green for Easter and served as a temptation for a little boy. It worked. Try as she might, my Grandmother could not convince me to give up the idea of taking that chick home. I suppose the person selling it must have supplied a box to carry it in and I am pretty sure we were close to home when we got it. I think maybe we were in Corsicana only a few miles from Malakoff. So, we took that cute little green chicken home to feed and water and watch it grow. Grow it did, and soon the cute little chick was replaced by a cantankerous rooster with a waddle, comb, and spurs. Anyone going into our backyard was immediately confronted by a fully grown beast who dared anyone to cross his path. If they did, they were met with a mad recklessly charging rooster, fully equipped with very sharp spurs and the will to use them. We soon learned to avoid this primal display by not venturing into the backyard. Visitors were fore warned and advised of our rooster's harmful intentions. One day the Farrells came to visit and my cousin John, who was about three or four, went into the backyard wearing short pants. Suddenly, without warning, that old rooster made his attack, flogging my cousin John on his legs and backside with those spurs and knocking him down into the sewer ditch. With John squalling, Grandmother screaming bloody murder, it sounded like someone was getting killed. They were. Granddad quickly surveyed the situation, reached into his pocket, opened up his knife, and slit the rooster's throat. We had fresh fried chicken for supper.

Several years later, again at Easter time, John's little brother Sam and little sister Trina saw a little green chick for sale where they stopped, while on the way to our house. Nothing would do but to get that cute little chick, so Aunt Martha reluctantly bought it for them and carried it to our house. When they were ready to leave, Aunt Martha convinced them it would be better if they left the chick for Granddaddy to take care of and they could pick it up the next time they came. Sam and Trina were not really happy to do so, but they finally agreed. Sam was eight and Trina about three. So, they looked forward to coming back in a few weeks to see their little green chicken. Several months passed before the next journey back to our house and by this time, that little chick was now a full-grown rooster. We all remember what the last one had done, so before he became mean, a remedy was secured. When Sam and Trina came back with the Farrells, guess what the meal was? Fresh fried chicken. They weren't told until years later they had eaten their pet.

COAL OIL RAGS AND CASTER OIL

Below is a poem I wrote, and it accurately describes the "good ole days" when no one went to the doctor and many home remedies were applied. If these failed a doctor might be called upon to make a house call.

Coal oil rags and Caster oil

Trying that Cold to foil

Sneezing, coughing, coughing,

Sneezing, blowing, blowing.

Nose all red.

Yes, you have a cold!!

You're back in the 1940's and

Grandma has a cure.

May work...but

It stinks... for sure!!

"Take this Caster Oil, Don

It'll make you all better!!"

"Then we'll put that coal oil rag.

Under your Shirt and sweater"

Off to school you go,

Smelling of where you've been

If stink counted, it'd be a sin!!

Oh, the good old days,

I can still taste it,

Smell it, remember it.

Coal Oil was a universal remedy for "purt near anything", as my Grandmother used to say. The sure cure for a cold was Caster Oil, which I still believe my Grandmother delighted in seeing my reaction to swallowing that awful stuff. The other thing used was a few drops of turpentine in a teaspoon of sugar, good for your cough. When someone had a scratch or a cut the answer was to pour Coal Oil on it. It is my belief Coal Oil, or kerosene as it is now called, is not the same as it once was. Coal Oil had universal usage; used in lamps, small stoves, for cleaning tools and treating chickens. If I developed a "chest cold" as diagnosed by my Grandmother, I needed a dose of Caster Oil and a Coal Oil rag on my chest. This was before penicillin and long before we would have gone to a doctor. This condition usually developed during the winter season when you put on extra clothes. There were no buses in those days and so the trip to school was made on our horses, our left and right foot. I always hated when my Grandmother "doctored" me and made me wear that awful yellow rubber raincoat. Before I was fully dressed in that awful raincoat my Grandmother insisted, I must have a Coal Oil rag on my chest, after the Caster Oil dose. The preparation always had the sequential steps. Heat lard in a pan, dip a rag in the hot melted grease, dip the rag in Coal Oil, using safety pins, pin the rag inside the undergarments so the rag is next to the chest. Often, I would still have the top to my jammers on and this is what the rag was pinned to, then I put on my long-sleeved shirt and subsequently added the raincoat if it even hinted of rain. With this all done, I was off to school, wearing this homemade remedy, stinking to "high heaven". Without the grease, I was always told the Coal Oil would burn me, but this was the least of my struggles. Trying to coax me to take Caster Oil was not an easy task once I had tasted that awful stuff. You would need to have first-hand experience to understand. I believe the taste was so awful it defies description. The first sign of the slightest cough out came that Caster Oil bottle and the spoon to cram it down my throat. I remember a story they told about my Granddad trying to coax my Dad to take Caster Oil when he was a little boy. My Granddad demonstrated for my Dad how there was nothing to it by taking some himself. After the first swig, Granddad said he would never give anyone that stuff every again, but my grandmother had no problem with making me take a dose. Years later, I found there may have been some actual good in taking a dose because the Caster Oil acted on viruses in the intestine which is the cause of many colds. The thing is, it's not the only thing in the intestine it acts on. It is also a good purgative. So now you not only stunk, but you also had the "green apple quick step". In other words, you were heading to the pot frequently. Remember, no indoor facilities were available. The closest out back was approximately 30 yards and if you ran, maybe you could make it without an accident. The alternative probably made more sense. Our indoor facility was a slop jar or porcelain pot. Years later I learned some of the things I was being forced to endure were declared carcinogenic or poison. In the case of the Caster Bean, a poison called Ricin can be derived from the bean and it is highly poisonous. In defense of my Grandmother, she was trying her best to help me not hurt me. If she had thought any of these remedies would hurt me, she would not have given them to me. Once my grandmother had given me my first dose of Caster Oil, I made up my mind.... NOT TO COUGH. If I did, I knew she would be grabbing that bottle which contained that stuff I so hated and trying to administer it to me again. Once again, the good Lord took care of me. There were other remedies somewhat less intimidating, but nevertheless, objectionable. If you were constipated there were remedies. Ex-Lax was a chocolate looking/tasting to get those bowels moving again. The other was the gum-like Fina-mint. Both of these worked pretty well and were not too harsh tasting. Then if you were really stove up, the old faithful, an enema. Grandmother said you needed this at least once a year, constipated or not. I am not going to go into gory details of how an enema works, if you are that interested, google it.

We had a couple of country docs who would make a house call on occasion. Dr. Kilman made several visits to our house. He would arrive in his 1940 something Cadillac and get out carrying his little black bag. This was likely after the home remedies had been tried and failed. I remember Dr. Rosenbloom came to our house to doctor me after one of my summer visits to Pt. Neches. He diagnosed my malady as Malaria and prescribed Quinine, which was bitter as all get out. At the time, we never questioned the good doctor, but over the years I have often wondered if I simply had a case of allergies.

An additional side note about Country Doctors making house calls. Trina, my Aunt Martha's youngest, stood in our front yard in Malakoff, playing with rocks. As she stood there, Dr. Kilman came by in his Cadillac, bound South to call upon a sick patient. Trina then about 5 years old, hurled a rock at his car and broke his windshield. She then quickly exited the scene. It wasn't until Aunt Martha answered the knock at the door that she knew of the incident. Apologies were made along with agreeing to pay for the damage. Ask Trina sometime about the whipping she got.

Sitting On the North Pole

If you have never been "lucky" enough to have an outdoor toilet, you don't know what you have missed. Maybe I should say, "You should be VERY glad you did miss it." An outdoor toilet is all most of us had when growing up in the late 40's and 50's. Ours was out a path about 30 yards behind our house. In the wintertime, my Grandmother would say, "I've got to go to the North Pole." And in the summertime, it was "going to Trinidad (a town 4 miles West of Malakoff)". Either way it meant she had to do #1 or #2. I am sure by this time the Days next door were already well equipped with indoor facilities, but not the Hendersons. I always wondered about Miss Willie across the street, but never enough of a wonder to explore the question. Next door, the Nokes were not originally modernly equipped, but finally were able to join the city folks. The city of Malakoff decided to put in a sewer line which ran through our yard, but the connection fee was more than we could afford, so when we did obtain indoor facilities, our discharge water ran through a ditch in the backyard. Before the ditch, all we had was a two-holer out back, with the location as stated above, either called The North Pole or Trinidad. Why we had a two-holer was never clear to me because in all the years I used it, never did two occupy that outhouse at the same time. I suppose it might have been so the poop could be evenly distributed on each side. In the winter there was nothing to stop that howling wind coming from the backside which faced west. It was COLD and sometimes bitter cold. On those days and of course at night, your better choice was the slop jar. In case you are not familiar, a slop jar was the most modern indoor apparatus if you had no toilet. The slop jar was approximately a 2-gallon porcelain lined metal bucket with a lid to be used when one could not go out back. The good thing about an outdoor toilet in the winter was the lack of critters. In the summer you were apt to find spiders, wasps, tumble bugs (they could be seen rolling a ball of poop along the ground), and plenty of flies. The flies were needed because they laid eggs in the wastes and produced worms which consumed the fecal material. The stink was there regardless of the season. There was no Johnson's Glade used back then, inside or out. We also did not have toilet paper, unless you count the Sears Roebuck catalog that was ever present in our outhouse. We called it our wish book because of all the neat items you could order from that catalog. While sitting, waiting for nature, it was a great time to browse. The use of a page out of that book left more than a little to be desired, but I'll bet most all poor folks used one. Charmin toilet tissue it was not. My other granddad, Granddaddy Tom Rogers, may have had the right idea. He told me, "Son, I would go to the barn, do my deed and use a corn cob to clean up with." I never tried his method, but it couldn't have been any worse on your rear than a page out of that Sears catalog. Inside the house an empty can which once held something like pork n beans might also be used if #1 was required. The slop jar or an empty can was kept under your bed in case of a necessity at night, especially in the winter. After we finally did get an indoor toilet, the only way to get to it was to go through my bedroom, so most everyone else still used the old method at night. Besides the indoor toilet, we now had a tub inside, whereas before, the #3 tub had to suffice for baths. A child or maybe even two could get into that #3 tub and have room, but it was way too small for an adult. This was a partial reason why baths were not as frequent as they should have been. One thing about it though, we did conserve water.

A story about my grandfather is a must to be included in this section. This story has been told in "Diary of a Backwoods Preacher" and it is one my grandmother always told in retaliation of one my grandfather told about her. In the old days, beds were kept higher than today's and things were easily stored underneath, including the slop jar. Late one night, Granddaddy had to relieve himself, so he pulled out the slop jar and began filling it. My grandmother woke and realized the sound was not of pee hitting in a slop jar. "Oscar, Oscar!" she cried. "You are peeing in your new hat!!" Well Granddad woke out of his stupor, realized what he was doing and stopped as soon as nature allowed. He ran to the window and threw the discharge out, trying to salvage that hat. Never knew if he did, but the damage was done, both to the hat and his pride.

The North Pole

It was on days like this

My grandmother

Called it the North Pole

And you had to be bold!!

Actually, out west

We trotted at our best,

No indoor facilities

Were we blessed!

Still remember I that path,

Out back; so far,

Either this; or,

The Slop Jar

A Sears Catalog

Awaited our plight

There you were …Out of Sight.

And the odors **that permeate**,

Caught **Your nostrils Only.**

No other had to suffer that fate.

If you've never been to the **NORTH POLE**

Then you are **NOT** among the

Old and Bold

ON THE NEXT PAGE, STANDING IN NOKES' FRONT YARD, ARE DON H. (HOLDING A DOG), RAY, EDDIE, PATSY, (HOLDING A FISHING ROD), ROYCE AND DON McClain

THE NOKES FRONT YARD

THE SOUTHSIDE GANG IN NOKES' FRONT YARD

Nokes Yard Games

The Nokes yard was a magnet for all sorts of games to be played. I suppose the earliest and most frequent was Eddie and I tossing the football to each other. Sometimes we used a real football and sometimes we even used a nerf ball. Tossing and catching for hours, always having fun. Ever present in the Nokes front yard was Mr. Nokes' brickyard truck. One day I ran out for a pass from Eddie, and I caught it, took one step and ran slap-dap into that truck. If this wasn't my first possible concussion, it was at the least the one I remember the most. That immovable truck did not budge one iota. I immediately collapsed in a heap beside the truck, knocked unconscious for an instant, while Eddie was laughing his head off. Had Royce been present he too would have been laughing. Basketball was played in Eddie's yard after a goal was put up. It was not a real goal, but one made from a hoop that was used to hold the staves of a wooden barrel together. It sufficed for giving us hours of fun. Much of the time we played tackle basketball since you couldn't really dribble anyway.

The Nokes acquired a Croquet set one summer and the new game in their yard was initiated. In those days, the balls and the mallets were real wood, not the modern plastic ones. The idea in case you are unfamiliar was to hit the ball through hoop, hit the post and continue to the next set of hoops until you made it all the way around. If an opponent decided to try and hit your ball with his, he/she was allowed to hold their ball with their foot, while it touched your ball, and then they could give a mighty swing with the mallet, sending your ball sailing into perhaps Mrs. Clay's yard or even into the road. About the time you thought you were about to transgress the entire circuit, some smart-alec would send your ball sailing. I am sure had we thought of it, we would have played tackle Croquet.

At night especially during the summer we played chase, and if you were "it", you had to chase until you were able to tag someone and then they were "it". Lokie, Eddie's little sister, was a Southside member, who participated in many of our Nokes' yard games. Rooster, Eddie and I and sometime Sammy, all played chase. I don't remember Royce being in any of these Nokes Yard chases. Every now and then we played chase in Eddie's yard using our bikes.

To add to the chase fun, we played "Kick the Can". The can was put in a circle drawn in the sand and the person who was "it" had to chase and touch someone in order to be relieved of the duties of guarding the can. While the "it" person was chasing, anyone could come in and kick the can out of the circle and then the "it" person had to retrieve the can and replace it in the circle before chasing could begin. All of our yard games consisted of little or no $, because none of us had any, but for sure, we had plenty of fun.

The Thing

In downtown Malakoff we had our own theater, The Victory, and it was here where all the kids in the town enjoyed movies especially on Saturday. The theater was not air conditioned, but air cooled, which was a lot cooler than being outside. I suppose The Victory got all of the latest movies, but it didn't really matter to us, as long as we were seeing a "shoot'em up" or maybe a Tarzan movie. Saturday was a must see because last week our hero was about to run off a cliff and we all just had to watch the rest of that serial to see if he made it. To get into the show it was going to cost you 9 cents if you under 12 and 14 cents of you over 12 and under 18, so on Saturdays, not only would you be able to see your favorite hero in the serial, but also you could see a cartoon, a comedy short, plus the regular movie, all in one day. You would come out, pupils dilated from the darkness, and red eyes due to several hours of film. Oh, yes, there was the news cast, also. If one happened to get into the show late as I did one day, until your eyes adjusted you could not see a thing. One day as a late arrival, I walked into that darkened movie house space, blinded. I walked down the aisle and proceeded to sit in an unoccupied chair. Only thing, it wasn't unoccupied. I sat squarely in the lap of some rather large gal, who screamed with an equally large voice and scared the be-jibbers out of me. I never knew whose lap I set in, but I knew I was a very unwelcome guest and quickly found an unoccupied seat. My later rules for late arrivals into a movie theater...." let your eyes adjust before trying to sit down".

One night during the summer a movie called "The Thing" was to show and from what Eddie and I had heard from friends it was scary. This prompted us to want to go see it and after we scraped up our 9 cents, which was not an easy task, we decided to go on a Friday night. Naturally we walked because that was the only method we had to get there. The Thing was about a giant alien creature that was what was described as a "giant carrot from outer space" and was found somewhere in the Artic region. That is about all I remember about the movie other than it was advertised as being scary, but nothing like that could be admitted by a card carrying Southside member, so even though both of us were scared during the movie, we each told the other after it was over, "Naw, that wasn't scary, I thought they said it was scary." And this is the way we began our walk home in the dark. I don't remember ever measuring the distance from downtown to home, but I figure it was about $1\ 1/2$ miles, nothing for us because we walked to elementary school, which was another half mile more from downtown, so we were used to walking, but not in the dark after seeing The Thing. As we walked along, we each heard a swishing noise that seemed to be right along with us, so we picked up our pace and so did the swishing noise. My heart was racing and I'm sure Eddie's was too. **Something** was following us and not only following, but **very** close. We both started running and so did that unknown **thing**, staying right with us. The faster we ran, the faster it did, until we finally frightfully arrived home. Eddie quickly ran inside while I skedaddled next door to my own house, and as I looked down, my eye revealed our pursuer....my shoestrings were untied.

Sand Games

There were lots of games we played in the sand. Like all young kids we made mud pies....and then ate them. Yuck. One game my cousin John and I played was with empty permanent wave solution bottles. These were discarded from my grandmother's beauty shop. They made fine little cars we could push on our imaginary roads we made in the sand. We didn't need any fancy toys to entertain ourselves, we created our own.

About the only tree shade in our yard was supplied by that same China Berry tree we stood under to have our China Berry fights. There was just enough shade to somewhat protect us from the hot sun and a plentiful supply of sand was underneath. The other shady location was in one side of our barn which had a roof over it and a dirt floor with plenty of sand. In the barn we could dig as many holes as we wanted to. It was a great place for us to play. This is where I dug a hole for a hiding place and used an old ice box door as my trap door. This place became my secret hiding place.

One sand game we played was with a critter which built a sink hole in the sand. The idea was to get down close to the hole and start yelling, "Doodlebug, Doodlebug, come out of your hole." This line was repeated several times. Soon you would see flicking of the sand coming out of the depression. Again, repeating over and over, "Doodlebug, Doodlebug, come out of your hole." I suspect the breath of our speech pattern vibrated the hole and this was an alert to the critter an insect was trapped, and a meal was forth coming. Watching for some unsuspecting insect like an ant falling into the crevice was fun. Once it fell in, there was no escaping, and it would soon disappear into the Doodlebug's trap. Years later we learned the Doodlebug was actually an Antlion, a larval stage of a winged insect much like a damsel fly or a lace wing. The antlion built its trap in the sand in order to catch insect and then devour them.

Everyone had a pocketknife back then, at least the boys did, and we always kept our knives sharp. A good pocketknife consisted of at least two, maybe three blades. The two-blade variety had one long and one short blade, while the one with a third blade was a leather punch used to put an extra notch in a leather belt that needed to be resized. We always needed our knives for something, like making arrows from the apple crates or maybe cutting out an old shoe tongue to be used for our slingshots. The knife was also handy for making rubber bands out of the bike inner tubes for our rubber guns. We all spent time sharpening them. Every boy kept a whet rock handy, and the blades would be sharpened by rubbing the blade in a circular motion on the rock. First a drop of machine oil was applied to the whet rock and then the circular sharpening motion would begin. If no oil was handy, spit would do. After the blade had been turned numerous times, it was time to test its sharpness. This was done by trying to shave the hair on your arm and if it failed it was back to the whet rock to repeat the process.

The other game Eddie and I played was Mumbly-Peg. Mumbly-Peg is a game played with a pocketknife and I am sure more than one set of rules exists, but Eddie and I had our own. A peg had to be constructed in order to begin the game. A good source was to use about a $1\,^1/_2$ in. long piece of a stick previously used as an arrow. Eddie and I used a pocketknife, having two blades. To begin the game, we took turns trying to score points with the flip of the knife. The knife was opened, and the long blade pointed straight out while the smaller blade pointed at a 90-degree angle. It was then held on the ground with the handle touching on one end and the smaller blade engaging the ground. The trick then was to flip the knife, trying to get it to stick in one of three position to score points. If the knife blade landed and stuck on the small blade, the person received 25 points. When it was flipped and the blade stuck with the long blade, this was worth 50 points, but if it stuck on both blades, the award was 75 points. We established a winning point total, like 400 points. We each took a turn until a winning total was reached, keeping score in our heads. The winner then was allowed to strike the peg one time with his knife with a mighty blow, driving it deep in the dirt. The loser had to pull it out with their teeth, which was impossible without getting a mouthful of dirt. Eddie claimed that I made him eat an awful lot of dirt.

Television in the 40's and 50's

The first television I remember seeing was at my Mother and Stepfather's in Pt. Neches Texas when I was eight years old. Every afternoon the neighborhood kids gathered at the Powers house to watch Howdy Doody Time. My sister, Vivien, was a magnet for all the kids in the neighbor anyway, but since my stepfather had one of the few TVs, the kids came for that. The summer of 1946 was the year I began visiting in Pr. Neches. Usually, I took part in games like canasta, monopoly, and sometimes I even tried jacks. I drew the line at jump rope, which all the girls played. I was a klutz at this. I would jump about twice and get my feet tangled, so I avoided that game. Howdy Doody was loved by all of Vivien's visiting friends, but not so much by me. Maybe it was because I was a couple of years older, I'm not sure. I did watch Howdy Doody because the television was something new and at times the peanut gallery was interesting to watch, but it was not my favorite pastime. Television was in its infancy then and there was maybe a maximum of two or three channels and very early in the evening TV would sign off and all you could see was a test pattern.

In Malakoff the first TV show I remember was watching wrestling next door at the Days. Charlie and Mable Day had the first TV in our neighborhood as far as I can remember, and they invited my Grandparents and me over to watch wrestling on Friday nights. It really was not wrestling, but rather "wrastling", which was about as fake as you could get, but my Grandmother thought it was real and maybe I did at the time. I remember Gorgeous George, one of the wrestlers, had long hair and would come out in the ring and spray perfume first. This thrilled the audience and also my Grandmother. There were several others, but their names escape me. There was always one good guy and one villain wrestling. Also there were tag team wrestlers and the two in the ring would battle each other until they tagged their partner outside the ring. The partner would then come in and go ahead to beat up the opponent. Sometimes one of the wrestlers would exit the ring and bring a folding chair back and start pounding the other guy with it. The main event took place after the TV part went off, so we had to go home and listen to the main event on the radio. The main event was often for the championship and the announcer would vividly describe the blow-by-blow action. Wrestling on TV was great entertainment, and we became regular Friday night guests of the Days. My Grandmother would really get into watching and she would cry out for them to stop that or quit that. It was as if she was a part of every blow. The wrestlers would sling each other into the ropes and then bounce off the rope and clobber the other guys. Although it was fake fighting, they were good at it. If you have ever witnessed a knock down drag out fight in a cowboy movie, then you would have an idea of how "wrastling" looked. It was the John Wayne type of fights and to our eyes it looked real, especially to my Grandmother.

The Dodsons' were the other family in our neighborhood with a television and once in the early 50's we gathered around their TV to watch a heavyweight boxing match between Joe Louis and Rocky Marciano. I don't remember much about the fight, but I do remember the TV bad reception. All televisions in those days received the signal with a tall antenna. A 3-inch diameter galvanized pipe at least 15-20 ft. tall was sunk into the ground and secured with four wire guidelines. The antenna was sunk in the ground directly next to the house and if a chimney was available, it ran alongside the chimney. That night the wind was blowing, so Dewey was outside with his monkey wrench trying to establish a good signal. Directions were given from inside the house while he turned the pole. "Can you see it now?" "No, keep turning clockwise." "Now that's better. Ok, a little more." "Ok, that's perfect." Then it would fade and again and Dewey would have to go back out and make more turns. The black and white picture was fuzzy with lots of static, but we were able to watch most of the fight. Other than the reception problems and the antenna turnings, the only thing I remember about the fight, Marciano won. In today's TV world, this match would have been on Pay for View, and I wouldn't even think about paying to watch it, but for these early Southside TV viewers, what a treat to able to watch a live heavyweight boxing match.

Our own family TV came by way of a deal my Grandmother made with Mr. Alton Chambers. His wife, Jo Chambers, would receive free hair work in My Grandmother's beauty shop in exchange for a television. We then had to hire the local TV expert, George Riddlespurger, to install an antenna alongside the house. We were excited to get our first TV made in Athens, Texas by Curtis Mathis. Mr. Chambers worked for Curtis Mathis, and he got the TV and put it in working order. The round screen on that TV was not more than 8 inches in diameter and the television weighed at least 40 or 50 lbs. For us it was a dream come-true. Television in our house for the first time!! We could receive a couple of stations from Dallas and maybe one from Tyler. Our picture was black and white, with static and fuzziness, but a picture none the less. The era of Television began full bloom in our house. My Grandmother could iron her clothes and watch. We were all enthralled by our new entertainment. We were able to watch some of the same things we had been listening to on radio; The Lone Ranger, Superman, Charlie McCarthy, and later: Gunsmoke, 77 Sunset Strip, Lucy, and several soap operas including "As the World Turns".

Stilts, Cans and Paddle Ball

Walking on stilts was loads of fun but required some dexterity and athletic ability. First the stilts needed to be constructed. Eddie and I decided the best way to do this was to find two 2 x 4's about 4 or 5 foot long. (an alternative method was to "borrow" the wooden handles off either an old shovel or hoe) The legs then needed to be equipped with a footrest placed within stepping distance of the user. In some cases, we put them high enough that the only way to mount the stilts was off a high object like maybe Eddie's porch. After a height was decided upon a 2 x 4 block about 4 inches long was attached perpendicular to the legs of the stilt, then a strap was placed running from the step block to the stilt leg. This could be made of rubber from and old inner tube or a piece of rope. The purpose of the rubber/rope was to keep the foot from coming out when you walked with the stilts. The next trick was to put a foot first in one of the "stirrups" then place the other foot in the other "stirrup", then begin walking. You had to walk straight legged. The easier method was to be on a porch or some higher place and put the left and right feet in the stirrups at the same time, then standing and walking. There was a real trick to this, and it took some practice. During the initial learning, falls were plentiful and Eddie, being stronger, learned to walk on stilts a lot quicker. Once you got moving, it became a matter of balance. After a while, we both learned to negotiate with those stilts. Being at least two feet off the ground proved to be lots of fun. The simpler way of doing this was to walk on cans that had been bent so your foot fit around them. Walking on the cans was easy; getting them to fit the foot was not. This can method did not elevate you, so it was not as much fun. I am fairly certain we got our idea for the stilts from either the Three Stooges or the Little Rascals. I remember seeing clowns on both shows walking on stilts. One way the stilts were used on these shows was someone walking around with pants matching the length of the stilts and having some sort of ad hanging front and back. These ad totters would walk the streets on stilts carrying their signs.

You know there was no way we could just walk on stilts without some game ensuing. After we both had made our stilts and became quite proficient with them, a fight while walking on stilts was our next adventure. This proved to be more dangerous than expected because when you fell, you fell farther and harder. This game soon was abandoned when we both decided this battle was going to get us hurt. Instead, we found an alternative game with four players, one a horse, the other a rider. In this activity, I rode on Royce's back and Rooster or Sammy road on Eddie's, the horses would charge each other and try to knock the other one down. The rider could grab the other rider and try to defrock them from their horse. Often both the horse and rider fell to the ground and sometimes only the rider when they were detached from their horse. Either way, this horsey game soon degenerated into block and tackle, with tempers sometimes flaring. This was another game Royce dreamed up for us to play. Another fine mess you got us into, Royce.

There were few games we played that did not evolve into a physical battle. Eddie and I made the FIRST cell phones by using a long string with a can on either end, one for me and one on the other end for Eddie. At a distance of about 50 feet, we would talk to each other...." Can you hear me now? .... Can you hear me now?" I am not sure we ever really heard each other though the string or if we just heard the voice, but we thought we did, and that was all that counted.

Paddle ball was another game we played not requiring hand to hand combat. In this game a paddle, in the shape of miniature tennis racket, only about 12 inches long and solid. The paddle was no more than 1/8 inch thick and attached to it was rubber band twenty or so inches long. The idea of this game was to hit the ball and the rubber band would spring out then hit the ball again when it came back. Our game for this was to see how many times we could strike and re-strike it without making a mistake. Out of all the games, Eddie and I played this was one I could almost beat him. To this day, I have wondered if this is what developed my hand eye coordination that I use in tennis. Eddie and I would spend hours trying to outdo each other with those paddles.

Annie-Over was another fun game we played. With this a ball was needed, usually a baseball, softball or a little rubber ball like used with jacks. Sometimes we used gloves and sometimes it was bare hands. In this game, one stood in either Eddie's or my backyard and when "Annie Over" was yelled the ball was thrown over the house. Ideally the ball after being thrown was caught by the other person and then a repeat happened in the opposite direction, with the use of "Annie Over." This was a simple game with low possibility of injury unless you barehanded it and hurt your finger or if you backed up and fell over something in the yard which was a possibility.

Lokie Nokes and I sometimes played volleyball 1 v 1 over our six-foot-high fence which separated our backyards. Using a large rubber ball, we would knock it back and forth until one of us missed. I still have a crooked little finger as a reminder of one of those games when Lokie spiked the ball on my left pinkie.

Kites, Gliders and Parachutes

March was the time when we built our kites because usually there was always a strong wind which was needed to have a good kite-fly. Being poor always demanded most of our fun things be built cheaply and with whatever we had available. It was no different when building a kite. You needed to make a cross-like structure for the center and then cover it with paper. The wood used needed to be light, but strong. If we had any arrow material left over, that was used. A cross was made by tying two sticks together such that the longer stick was on the vertical. In the Henderson household we had paper shades you could pull up and down. This was what all poor people used who couldn't afford those fancy venetian blinds. At bottom of these shades was a perfect kite making stick or for my grandmother a perfect switch when she needed to whop me or John for a quick little spanking. One day she went to grab one to administer a paddling to me (which I am sure I deserved) and when she reached to get the "paddle" there was none there, so now she was doubly mad and knew very well where it had disappeared; now, back to the kite building. The horizontal crosspiece needed to be bowed with a string, making it like you would for a bow and arrow. A string was then run around the outside forming a nice diamond shape. Next the skeleton kite was covered with paper, usually old newspaper or the best kind was a sack from Hardy's cleaners originally used to protect a recently cleaned and pressed suit. A quick visit to the closet to "borrow" that cleaning sack without permission because it was being used to protect Granddad's freshly cleaned and pressed suit. The paper was then placed on the out-bow side and glued in place using a paste made of flour and water. Flour and water make a good glue and will hold the paper in place. A bridle for the kite needed to be made and this was a string on the out-bowed side running along the vertical stick. Several attempts to get our kite in the air resulted in dismal failure until my Granddad told us we needed a tail, the longer the better. An old bed sheet was then ripped into strings that could be tied together and another launch was tried. The end of a spool of string was tied to the center cross string and while holding the kite with one hand and the string in the other an attempt was made to fly the kite. You had to make a running start and allow the wind to lift the kite into the air and once in the air, let the string flow off the spool and up she would fly. We quickly learned you needed plenty of room, and our front yard didn't work as well as evidenced by several kites caught on electric wires running parallel to the road and just across the street. So, it was to Robertson's open field where there were no wires or trees. When everything went right that kite would be carried to great heights and it would stay up as long as we wanted or until in some cases, the ball of twine might slip out of our grip and go sailing and the kite with it. It was then the chase began especially if the wind was really strong. I would find myself running after that ball of twine as it skipped along the ground, unwinding, as the wind suddenly pulled the kite and the ball of string farther and farther away from me. If I was lucky, I caught it before the kite crashed to the ground. The kite would begin dipping and start to go in a circle like a wounded buzzard and unless I could grab the twine and pull it taut again, I would need to start all over again, re-launching the crashed kite. I am sure the store-bought kind of kite would not have cost more than a quarter, but that was a lot of money then. With a quarter you could go to the movies, have popcorn and a drink and still have a penny left for bubble gum, so the Southside members always built their own.

Everyone learned to fold paper and to make a good paper airplane. Often times this was done in the classroom when the teacher left the room. Someone would sail a paper plane and it would glide across the room. These paper planes often had various designs and some sailed and some crashed, but we all tried what we thought was the ultimate sailing design. I am not even going to try to tell you how we folded those paper planes, for one thing, I have forgotten. I do remember some would be designed to glide for a long distance, some to go around in a circle, some with sharp points to hit someone and a mired of other designs.

One time my Uncle Frank brought me a store-bought balsa wood glider when the Farrells came to visit. This was the real deal. Unlike the paper airplane which might or might not fly, that balsa wood glider would glide forever and if the wings were adjusted slightly differently it would even glide in circles. Of course, balsa wood is a fragile material and apt to be easily broken. Many hours were spent flying that glider and many more gliders were flown after this. I am sure that glider didn't cost any more than a dime or at most a quarter, but what fun it was.

I learned that some of my friends were building their own model airplanes out of balsa wood. These kits came with all of the pieces needed to build a model airplane. These pieces were then cut out or punched out and finally glued together. The kit came with instructions detailing exactly how to put the model together and if you followed these instructions you could end up with a fine model of some vintage airplane made to scale. I never could follow those directions and several bought models were never finished. Just think my Dad, Albert, using only his pocketknife and scrap pine, carved and put together a model airplane, which I still have. I couldn't even build a store bought one.

It was also during the time when model airplanes were being built people began placing little engines in them. So, when I saw an ad in my Boy Scout magazine listing a model airplane engine for sale, this made me want to build and fly one. I ordered it with the intent of building a model from scratch, inserting that motor, and flying it. Now, almost 70 years later, I still have that "never used" model airplane motor.

One simple toy we made was a parachute. When I was six years old, living in Abernathy, Texas, my friend Lane Tannehill and I were celebrating the end of WW II. I suppose the war had ended and we apparently knew of it. Lane, during the celebration, threw down the leg supporting a toy machine gun and that leg bounced up hitting me in the head. I was immediately screaming bloody murder and bleeding profusely. If you have ever dealt with a head cut, you will know how they bleed. It was a trip to the doctor and my Aunt Martha took me, and I was squalling like a pig under a gate. I must have had blood everywhere and I did not want that doctor touching me, so I screamed and cried even harder. Aunt Martha had received a gift from her husband, my Uncle Frank, who was still in the military. I had previously seen this gift and wanted to play with it, but my Aunt firmly denied me this privilege because it was a special gift. The gift was a little doll dressed in an aviator uniform with a parachute attached. Thrown into the air, the little soldier would float to the ground supported by his parachute. I wanted that doll as soon as I saw it. In order to stop my crying, my Aunt Martha said, "Don, stop crying and I'll give you the parachute doll." After I heard this, my agitated crying digressed to merely a sob or two. A few stiches later and home with a bandage on my head, her promise was confirmed. The last I saw of that little doll, it was hanging from an Abernathy electric wire. The rest of the story; Lane Tannehill is the grandfather of NFL and former A&M quarterback Ryan Tannehill. It is indeed a small world, for I had not seen or heard from Lane since we moved away, shortly after this incident. This is the way I was first introduced to a parachute, and it served as the pattern for making a homemade one. Granddad would not miss one of his handkerchiefs, so I borrowed one and tied on four strings, equal length, on the four corners, then attached a washer where the four strings came together. Bingo, a parachute!! Hours of fun were had throwing up this homemade parachute and watching it float to the ground, but then one day.... that wire captured another of my toys. Another one could be easily made, and I did. That wire which ran parallel to the road in front of our house was starting to be decorated with lost toys; a kite, a couple of parachutes, a sling shot and no telling what else that wire had captured.

Willie Romine

Willie Romine was one of those characters in Malakoff, Texas with whom I found a great deal of fascination and so did everyone else in town. Willie (I never knew if he had any other name) was a small wiry guy who stood about 5 foot 4 inches if he stretched. Willie was usually dressed in those old khakis clothes, the ones with long sleeves, and always that flop hat. Willie, besides being a bootlegger, was thought of as the town's idiot (don't know how else to describe it). To make a living, other than bootlegging, he would plow gardens for people, using his mule. No one could ever say that Willie was lazy. He plowed our backlot several times and he always did an excellent job. During the summer after Willie finished plowing a garden, you could find him at the Tiger Inn, buying a double dip Vanilla Ice Cream cone. This was a regular thing which he loved to do. Maybe one of the few pleasures he had.

The other thing he did was to haul trash for people. He may have used that same mule to pull a wagon to collect the trash, I can't remember. He had picked up our trash more than once and it never occurred to me to think about where he put the trash. At the time, Malakoff had no dump yard that I know of, but Willie dumped it, nevertheless. One of my early entrepreneur endeavors was selling garden seed. I would walk around town and knock on doors, asking if the owner wanted to buy any seeds. This is when I learned where Willie Romine took the trash. It was to his house, and it was stacked around his house, on the sides, in the back, up front and all around. It was an adventure just getting to the front door. When I finally found the way up and knocked on the door, Mrs. Romine answered. Very nice lady and not the kind I would have matched with Willie, but none the less, she was, and I felt sorry for her. She bought some flower seeds and I wondered at the time, "Where in the world is she going to plant these?" because I never saw any opening for a flower bed.

One Sunday, Willie visited our Church, and he even had on clean clothes. My Granddad and he were near the same size but that is where the comparison ended. At some time or the other, Willie must have read and learned bible passages because he began spouting scripture to my Granddad in an effort to get into a debate with him. I was surprised at how much scripture Willie knew, but he was no match for my Grandfather, which Willie soon learned. He came back to Church several times, each time seeking another debate, which in my opinion he lost again. Years later I learned Willie had used similar tactics in other Malakoff Churches. On the one hand Willie seemed crazy, but on the other hand, he was quite smart.

My other Granddad, Tom, told me stories about Willie which gave me clues as to why he was the way he was. Granddaddy Tom told me that Willie had a big mean brother-in-law liked to use his discrepancy in size and beat up on Willie. The brother-in-law delighted in doing this on a regular basis. One day while Willie was plowing a field, the brother-in-law appeared in the field and started toward Willie. Willie was prepared and had enough of getting beat up. Willie brought an axe with him, and he warned the Brother-in-Law that if he came any closer, he was going kill him. The Brother-in-Law laughed and kept coming. They might not have charged Willie with manslaughter if he had stopped at the first axe swing (which killed the brother-in-Law), but Willie kept hacking until the Brother-in-Law was cleaved into pieces. Willie was convicted of murder and sent to Huntsville State Prison. From everything my Granddaddy Tom told me it was pure case of self-defense. It was those added chops that probably sent him up. I have never been able to confirm the rumor of how Willie was released from prison, but I'll tell you what I heard. Back in the old days, Huntsville State Prison held a once-a-year rodeo with bare back riding, bull riding, roping and etc. This story could be another rumor, but it was told to me as follows. If an inmate was able to stay on a certain bull for a certain time, that inmate would be released from prison, and Willie did just that. Even if part of Willie's prison story is true, we can understand why Willie had an unbalanced mind, perhaps even to the point of making him a bit crazy. The bootlegging that Willie did was a matter of fulfilling a need for the local drinkers, who could not otherwise buy any liquor close by because Malakoff was dry at the time, meaning no one, legally sold alcohol. Another rumor said Willie often went to Houston and it was thought he would hitch a train or thumb it. No one ever knew why he went to Houston, but he was killed by a train, somewhere between Malakoff and Houston and was found with a large amount of cash on his person. Some even said he was working for the CIA as an undercover agent, which I have serious doubts about. Nevertheless, one of Malakoff's more illustrious characters was no longer with us.

Dodd's Lake

Melvin Dodd was a small-time gangster who resided in Malakoff during prohibition days. The infamous Tavernale was owned by Melvin, and this was the local speakeasy during the 1920's and '30's. He was also connected with illegal stills being run in Henderson County. It was rumored law enforcement turned a blind eye to Dodd's activities because they had their palms crossed with a bit of cash. In the 1950's, Melvin Dodd became legitimate and built a lake, known as Dodd's Lake northeast of Malakoff. The lake was stocked with fish and surrounding the lake Dodd built cabins for rent. Somewhere on the property was a landing field. There was a swimming area with a beach and out about 200 yards were two diving boards and a slide. On the beach a covered area for sitting was provided. You could pay to swim and dive or just to sit and watch. Paddle boats were for rent. The paddle boats were a one-man floater having paddle boat fins on the back. This was driven by peddling it like a bike. Someone said Melvin invented these, but anyway, he was now 100% legitimate as far as I know. In addition to the lake a skating rink was also available. Dodd's Lake became a fun attraction for both young and old. It was a hangout not for only local teens, but those from every surrounding area. Dodd's Lake became a thriving recreational location and the Southside gang, who had long outgrown The Inch Pond, soon became frequent swimmers in Dodd's Lake. We sacrificed the cool blue waters and the privacy of our Inch Pond for the crowds which flocked to Dodd's Lake. I truly missed our Inch Pond, not only for the cooler and prettier water, but for its secluded and almost private nature. I am reminded of the Charles Atlas ads which read, "Don't let the bullies kick sand in your face! Learn how to become a Charles Atlas!!" Not the exact words I am sure, but it was in all the magazines advertising for you to order your Charles Atlas course and build up your muscles so that you would not have sand kicked in your face. So, skinny Don would rather have gone swimming in our little private pond, hidden from most eyes. There was no sand to kick there and no one to make fun of my skinniness. Royce on the other hand loved Dodd's Lake because he could show off his physique, which was more like Charles Atlas's. Over the years, Royce had learned to dive and to do some pretty elegant dives like a jackknife, a swan, and even a $1\,^1/_2$ from the high board. I could do some pretty good "cannon balls" from the high board, and maybe a sort of a jackknife. During my summer visits to my Mother's in Pt. Neches I had given their public swimming pool a try and had learned a few dives. My Stepfather, Paul, loved to go swimming and he had taken me to a public pool in Beaumont where I had learned a few more dives. As always if Royce dared you to do something, you were compelled to do so, and diving was no different. I practiced during my summer visits to Pt. Neches in hopes of being good enough to meet Royce's challenges which would be forthcoming. Then one day while at Dodd's Lake, that challenge came. When Royce did a 1 1/2, he said, "Come on, Don, you try it!" I wanted to be able to show him that I could. While attending Lamar Tech in Beaumont I found myself without a summer job and lacking a P.E. credit, so I enrolled in a swimming class to satisfy my requirements. It was a course designed to teach you different swimming strokes and safety in the water. The instructor was Ty Terrell, the Lamar head track coach. I don't remember him ever getting into the water, instead he instructed us from poolside. After the class instruction there was ample time to practice a few dives, so I took advantage of it, knowing that high dive and Royce's challenge awaited me at Dodd's. Sure enough, that time came during the summer. I have been trying to think of the year, but I could not come up with anything other than a guess. It was about 1959 or 1960 and I was living in Pt. Neches and commuting to Lamar college. A summer visit to Malakoff allowed me the opportunity to meet the challenge for which I had been practicing. There was Royce up on that high board at Dodd's and making his routine spring and then jumping. First, he did a classic Jackknife as I watched. As he entered the water, there was barely a splash. Typical Royce, always good at anything he tried. I am not certain the height of that board, but it was very high. The only dives I had ever done off it were cannon balls or a rather poor jackknife, but I had been practicing in the Lamar pool and I felt confident that I could show Royce I had learned how to dive. Royce climbed back to that high dive performing a $1\ 1/2$ with ease. If judges had been there, they would have awarded him at least an 8.5 or better. Royce then issued his challenge, "Ok, Don, can you do that?" I didn't say anything, but just began climbing that ladder, nervous, but knowing I could at least do a $1\ 1/2$, not as well as Royce, but nevertheless a reasonable facsimile. I took my bounce and then hit the end of the board, making my turn in the air and landed in the water for a perfect $1\ 1/4$ directly on my left ear. That not only ended my swim/diving for the day, it ended my summer Swimming Course at Lamar. When the doctor in Pt. Neches looked at my ear, he reported that I had basically blistered my eardrum with little blisters all over it. Yes, I did not chicken out, Royce, but another fine mess I let you get me into. Now almost 60 years later, I still have hearing loss in my left ear. After my failed dive, Royce only laughed When he saw that I really was hurt, he felt bad. This was my last response to a diving challenge by Royce or anyone else.

The Dodd's Skating Rink

In April of 1957, Melvin Dodd opened a state-of-the-art air-conditioned skating rink. This was an addition to the already popular Dodd's Lake and offered both teens and adults a great place to skate. People came from all over, but especially from Malakoff and Henderson County. If I had ever skated before, I don't remember it. I had heard stories about my Dad and Uncle Preston skating. At one time a rink was located on what is now highway 31 at the intersection of the road to Caney City. My Grandparents, Dad, Uncle and Aunt lived in a house which later became the location for Kilman's hospital. Directly south, across the highway from their home, was the roller rink where my Dad, Albert and my Uncle Preston became frequent visitors and very good skaters. My Dad was a fancy skater while Uncle Preston was the speed skater. The reason I chose to discuss my Dad and my Uncle is because I thought, "Well, if my Dad and Uncle were good skaters, I must have some of the same talents." It was with this valuable information that I set forth to utilize my genetic inheritance. Boy was I wrong. Not only was I wrong, I wasn't even close. I was flat out terrible and not only dangerous to myself, but even more so to the other skaters. The first thing you should learn to do is how to stop, well, I couldn't. It was like an awkward duck coming in for a landing and everything on the runway better clear. If you have ever watched the

Honeymooners in one episode where Ralph tries to skate, that was me. I could not stand up on those skates without falling on my Butt and I could not stop when I needed to. Skating around in a circle was a real disaster because I was an accident waiting to happen. Eventually when Don got on the floor, an announcement was made, "Look out Henderson is on the floor!" I couldn't blame them. Some have said they were scolded by certain "Church" people for skating with a girl. Why? Because it was a sin the way they held each other. I never had to worry about this because no girl in her right mind would have ever skated with me. How I kept from breaking an arm or some other body part was a pure miracle. Once again, God took care of me.

Four and Twenty Blackbirds

Remember the nursery rhyme,

Sing a Song of Six Pence

Sing a song of sixpence,
A pocket full of rye.
Four and twenty blackbirds,
Baked in a pie.
When the pie was opened
The birds began to sing.
Wasn't that a dandy dish?
To set before a king

This is the way I remember reciting it, but it has been a while, so all of the words might not be correct. Please pardon me if I have strayed from the original, but the words, "Four and Twenty Blackbirds, baked in a Pie", were the words that caught mine and Eddie's attention. In the springtime, when fields were ploughed for planting, the sky would be filled with blackbirds flying overhead or there would be a large flock lit in a recently ploughed field. Eddie and I decided that if we killed some blackbirds, we could bake them and make a pie, so that's what we did. I don't remember how many we shot; I know it wasn't four and twenty, maybe four. We gutted and cleaned them, anticipating a blackbird pie. In my backyard we had the perfect spot to cook. Formally it had been used to heat water in an iron pot for the purpose of washing clothes. This provided the area needed to build a fire for cooking our dressed blackbirds, so we set out to cook them in a large pot borrowed from my Grandmother's kitchen.

Eddie and I were all excited, thinking the blackbird pie was going to taste really good. We knew that the birds would not sing, but we were still in hopes it might be a dandy dish "to set before a king". To this day I still can taste my bite of those blackbirds. Yuck!! It was disgusting to say the least. It might have worked for four and twenty, but it didn't work for just four. Eddie had the same reaction and that ended our blackbird culinary delight.

Comic Books

One of our favorite pastimes was reading comic books. We called them "funny books", and some were funny, but many were Adventure Books like: Superman, Batman, Plastic Man, Green Arrow and the Lone Ranger. Oh, if only we had kept some of those copies. The funny ones were Little Lu Lu, Archie, and....??? Eddie Nokes and I often exchanged funny books and so did Don and Delores McClain who lived south of us. Those books had the HIGH price of....10 cents!! In those days it was not easy to scrape up a dime. One way was to sell cold drink bottles at Kirby's for 2 cents (this is what we called any Bottled drink ...Soda water is a Yankee term) The only problem with that .... we didn't have money to buy a cold drink to begin with, so this limited our buying comic books.

In my household we could not afford a newspaper and therefore we did not get the Sunday funnies. My alternative to this was to listen to a Tyler radio station on Sunday mornings before going to church. The radio announcer would read and describe in detail each comic strip and I would listen with attentive ears. They always announced that you could send in a postcard with your name and address and win 20 comic books, so I sent in a postcard. Lo and behold, I won!! I have often wondered if perhaps not only was I the Only one who entered, but perhaps the only one listening. I was thrilled to learn that I had won. That was a whole $2 worth of comic books. Wow!! I remember among the books there was at least one Superman. This winning was in the late 1940's or early 1950's. All of those books have been lost long ago, but I have often wondered if among that group, one of those .10 cent books may have been worth a bunch. Eddie Nokes had a book about WWII airplanes that I always had my eye on, and I talked him into swapping my comic books for his airplane book. Long gone are the comic books as well as that airplane book.

Wheaties and Post Toasties

During the late forties and early fifties our cereal choices consisted of: Wheaties (the breakfast of champions), Post Toasties, and Cheerios. These cereals always had a lure for kids like me. Not for the cereal, but rather neat prizes you could get. With a box top and a small fee, you could send off for some type of neat toy. This was right up my alley, and I was enticed to order something like a secret decoder ring or a Lone Ranger miniature gun ring. On that gun ring was something like a cigarette lighter and when you turned the wheel, sparks were emitted. Some cereals held a prize within them, and every box had something different. I still have one of those prizes.... a Kats and Jammer Kids ring. The long wait for the ordered item was almost too much for my eager mind.

My Grandmother's Nose

My Grandmother, Grace Roberts Henderson, weighed about 85 lbs. wearing her winter coat and carrying her purse. It is with this description that I present to you what one can do when fear causes adrenaline to kick in. Late one night I woke to the sound of my Grandmother yelling, "Fire!". Later I learned she had awakened smelling smoke and it was coming from the cabinet that housed our silverware and cup towels. When she opened the cabinet door, smoke began pouring out and she grabbed up the smoldering towels, pulled them out, then beat on them with a towel, putting out a what could have been a serious fire. Because my Grandmother's highly sensitive nose, she prevented an otherwise serious mishap.

Another time my Grandmother smelled smoke and she decided it was coming from the next-door neighbor's garage. Quick as a wink, she rushed to where she thought the smoke was originating only to find a padlock on the door. My 85-pound Grandmother grabbed the lock and tore the lock, screws and all off in a single mighty jerk. How she did this can only be attributed to brute strength supplied by a rush of adrenaline. She found the fire inside and put it out probably not only saving the garage, but perhaps the neighbor's house as well as ours. Thank you, God for Grandmother's nose!!

Polk Salad

I grew up with an East Texas spring tradition that I am continuing today in Spring, Texas. Every spring my Grandfather would gather some fresh Polk Salad leaves and my Grandmother would cook them. She never had a recipe for anything so I never knew exactly how she fixed the Polk (not that I would have paid any attention anyway) All of you young people out there you should write down those recipes now if you want to remember them later. Polk was not one of my favorites, but my Grandmother would always insist that I needed my "spring tonic". She made it in an iron frying pan, and I know she used lard (what else did we fry with?) and there were scrambled eggs in it. Like many other "tonics", it was best eaten by choking it down (at least for me). I was never a fan of any "greens"; much less the "wild" variety. A few years ago, a plant came up in our backyard and I recognized it as Polk Salad. I thought I would try some if I could find how to cook it. Looking on the internet, bingo, guess what I found. Polk is poison!! Really!! Add that to Caster Beans, Coal Oil (Kerosene), turpentine and a lot of other things my grandparents made me ingest for health remedies!! I learned that the Indians used Polk as did many of our early Texas settlers. Why not, it grows free, but poison???? All of the articles stated that you needed to par boil it first and I wasn't even sure what that meant. When you reach a certain age, you must rely on someone that is still around that would know, but alas, all are gone. My wife's side were Yankee city folks, so they "don't know nothing"!! Left to my own ingenuity and bravery, I collected leaves and "par boiled" them. I placed the leaves in a pan then covered with water and boiled, then poured off the water. I did this three times. ...Sounds somewhat like some of my Organic chemistry labs in college. From there it was guess work with the eggs. Well, I tried eating it and it wasn't any worse than what I remembered. I lived. Not poisoned. No one else in the family would even taste it. My son took one look and emphatically said, "I am not eaten any of that crap"!! OK, I remember those sentiments!! It was several years before I braved this again; but this spring, up sprouted another Polk in the backyard. Maybe I should have allowed my son to mow it down, but instead I yelled at him (when he volunteered to mow my yard), "Don't mow that plant!!" "Why not, that's just an old weed!!" "That's Polk Salad!", I said. "So???" he said. I decided to pick a few of the smaller leaves and placed them in water and after a few hours I put them in the refrigerator in a baggie. After several days of contemplation, I finally decided that I wanted to cook them. It was lunch hour, the day of my tennis match and I thought, "What if I get sick from eating this"? But I surged forward, using my own recipe: Par boil the leaves three times and pour off the liquid each time. Add at least a cup and a half of Beef or Chicken Broth in with the leaves and cook until tender. It actually tasted pretty good.

Golfing with the Farrells

Each holiday, while I was in college, and after I graduated, the Farrells and I would play golf in Tyler or Athens. Uncle Frank and I were usually partners against Sam and John. Uncle Frank was an excellent golfer having a professional looking swing. He could drive the ball a mile and chip and putt with the best. I, on the other hand, was a real hacker. Sam could drive the ball a mile and was a good putter and chipper. Sam was capable of shooting near par. John was an accurate driver, a good putter and could also shoot near par. The two teams would be set to battle with some small side bet. Our rules were simple; the partners with the lowest score won the hole. It would be seldom that I would ever win, but sometimes I might help tie. Over the years we had some very competitive games mainly because every now and then Uncle Frank would chip one in or sink a long putt. John and Sam would gasp and exclaim, "Dang Daddy, he did it again!!" If Uncle Frank chipped or putted one in and it was sheer luck and Not skill, Uncle Frank didn't even want to take the point. One time when he was in a tournament, he accidentally chipped one in and because he did, even though his shot had won the tournament, he conceded to the other guy because he didn't want to win with an accidental chip in. Uncle Frank grew up in Ft. Worth and was a star football player for Northside High school. He would practice golf when he got a chance and was very good at it. He was a perfectionist. Some of the greens he played on were not greens at all, but rather sand and oil. Putting was difficult on this type of green, so he developed his chipping in order to get as close to the hole as possible. Uncle Frank might have played college football at TCU had WWII not come along. My Uncle left these links in 1992.

Ode to Uncle Frank

By Don Henderson

Never again to be the same
Challenges are gone.
To play the Game

Uncle Frank is gone from these
Links on earth,
But it was he who first encouraged
this game and taught us its worth.

The challenge of the game
still remains out there
But not the same as when
Uncle Frank was here.

Days aren't the same, Challenges gone,
Why shoot a good score
Without Uncle Frank to analyze
and analyze some more.

Always I forward looked to holidays.
And Summer's late
Golf game mentioned to Uncle Frank.
He'd never hesitate.

Sometimes we all played, the Farrells and I,
That was the most fun.
Not the score, Nor who won.

Instead, the one shot to be.
Remembered and bragged about.
To beat Uncle Frank,
Inwardly we vowed.

Even after he aged and limped
As we played
He still had that one shot that left us.
Oft amazed

Just when we thought we had him.
Down a stroke,

He'd chip one in and
Grin and joke

Always a perfectionist
On the course about the game.
 If you didn't play pure, he put you to shame.
 Then there was his putting,

 Remember this.

When he really needed to make it,
he would rarely miss.

Through the years I've saved and kept the Cards of score,
In hopes in future years to conjure up Memories more
As these I pick up, and review contents.
Mementos and memories flow,
'membranes of Past events

When Uncle Frank was on
The Golf course, it was his stage,
Sometimes his pulpit, and sometimes
His rage.
It's hard to find a real game
These days   the same challenge is past,
As once we did gage.

Work, family, time and events,
Now keep us apart,
But the same game now
Is a different sort.
Only memories of past episodes,
Keep our minds vividly alert.
But just as lost balls.
Lost lives, we cannot avert.

So, as we still continue to play the
Game of life on earth let us remember, as in golf,

Not the score, but the challenge
Supplies us our worth!

I salute the memories of
My playing pal and Uncle
Who gave me the game of
Golf and more.
Challenged to make one last shot,
One last putt, One last drive, one last score.

Thanks Uncle Frank for the game to us you gave,
Thanks for being a competitor in life,
Showing us all, that in golf,
as in life always there's strife.

But in the end to remember.
Linger and Cherish the best shots,
the best Lines
the best Putts,
the best Times

Your nephew and playing partner, Don Henderson
Copyright by Don Henderson October 15, 1995
Uncle Frank left these Earthly links in 92.

The following poem was written after one of the Southside members; Billy Joe (Toothpick) Robertson left this Realm. Because Malakoff was a small community, we knew everyone, and it was much like having an entire town made up of kin folks.

OUR LIFE IS LIKE A TREE

By Don Henderson 5/22/14

When someone leaves this Realm,
Having been set free,
It always makes me think of
Our life as a tree.

A tree, having many branches;
Each a person whose life we shared.
A tree, alive with many
Branches undercover,
All intertwined

In one way or the other
I see the Tree of
The Malakoff Family
And her Branching History

Remembering that we
All were once little sprouts,
Leaflets you see,
But all connected
All part of that Family Tree
For some, sadness came early;
Their leaves and branches Fell free, unable to
Continue this life's Journey.

As our tree grew older,
Many limbs; fragile hung
We began to realize
More to be lost,
Was yet to come.

Because this
Malakoff Tree Lives
Each Limb Lost,
Hurts us all
Knowing not
The next to fall

Our Family tree will Continue
On this Earthly Land.
Each branch precariously clinging
Knowing Destiny ultimately
Lies in God's hand

But, we know, As long as we are
Rooted in his love,
Though a branch is lost to us
God gathers them
For his forest above

THE OLD ROCK SCHOOL

Several years ago, our old Rock School was about to be torn down. This was the elementary school many had attended. The school board voted to tear it down and build a new school, but suddenly there were protests. For many of us tearing it down was not acceptable. The school was built by the WPA during the depression using rocks. The school had served the community for many years and now it was on the chopping blocks ready to be demolished. But due to the outcry ultimately prevented this. I am proud to say the Old Rock School has been saved. The following is a poem about that school building. It was written as a tribute to our memories with hopes of saving the old school.

By Don Henderson written July 15, 2009,
Can be sung to "Rock of Ages"

Rock School of Ages, please stay with me
Let me bind, myself to thee

Let the people, who've grown cold,
Remember when, your halls,
once overflowed

Back us then, for double sure
Remove from them, their MISTAKEN CURE

With the labor, of public hands
Once fulfilled, our town's demands

Keep our zeal, for the school we know
Else our tears will, forever flow.

Rock school of ages, cling to thee
Let us keep, our memories

Built with rock, so carefully,
Built to last, eternally

Tear her down, you say to me;
Worthy to stand, you must agree.

Save our school, our rock elementary
Don't tear away, our memory

Years have come and gone;
Many friends and loved ones, passed on

The Old Rock School, meant for many
Pursuit of life and memories a-plenty

Rock school of ages, we cling to thee
Let us save you, for all posterity!

SHE IS SAVED!!!

**THANKS TO ALL WHO WORKED
TO SAVE HER**

Last Run to Glory

By Albert Don Henderson

May of 2000

The thrill of watching a touchdown excites everyone, including me, especially if the T.D. involves number one. As I lined up in the backfield, I could hear music. I could hear distant muffled yelling on the sidelines that seemed almost unreal. Concentrating on the task at hand; I had told myself, OK, you've got to see the field, don't run into someone, don't fumble, don't fall down. Come on legs, don't give out." My heart raced as I thought about the run. I could hear pounding in my ears and tightness in my chest. All of this was reminding me that maybe I should have just said, "No", but there was no backing out now. My quarterback had announced, "Quick, count!" I suppose everyone else knew what this meant. I was thinking, "Is he going to say, down, set, set, or just down?" I wanted to ask but didn't. My mind began to wander and ponder about too many things. Did I pull something when I warmed up in the locker room? Would I be able to run in "full uniform"? My quads felt very tight. Earlier that afternoon, I had spread my-o-flex from just above my waist halfway to my ankles. My wife saw me and wanted to know if my hemorrhoids were hurting. I said, "Yea, but this is my-o-flex to loosen my muscles. My hams were really tight. We had made the practice run on Friday and I'll tell you this. Practice may make "perfect", but practice "once" makes you very sore. As we were doing our usual chores on Saturday, I reflected to my wife that I was concerned about mowing the lawn. I might hurt my back before the game that night. She graciously agreed to mow so I would not get hurt. (I should have thought of this before!) I was now aware that Montgomery, the quarterback, was barking signals. I stood half crouched, almost chimpanzee like. "Oh! I think he called the play!" Come on legs don't fail now. Brain heard, but my feet didn't. Remember the coaching. "Left elbow up, right hand underneath. Take the hand-off, don't fumble. Go right. (Don't fall down! Don't drop that ball!) Then I was off. I forgot about "seeing the hole". Hey, I didn't really see anything. I was aware that I had the ball, and that I was supposed to keep my legs pumping. I tried that. It felt like I was standing still in thick, waist deep mud. I was quick... the first 15 yards. A vague awareness of bodies around caused me to elude several ghost-like figures groping in the dark for me. I floated, dream-like, without really seeing. It was as if a thick fog surrounded everything. My glasses fogged up. Avoiding almost invisible pursuers, more by accident than planning; I crossed through the thick fog. Am I ever going to reach the goal line? An eternity passed. Finally, I "outran" all of my would-be tacklers and crossed the goal line. Before the game, suggestions had been made about how I should act after I scored. A "White Shoes Johnson" dance with a fancy waggle? Everything became blurred. I started to kneel, changed my mind, spiked the ball and then kneeled. By this time, I could see again. It was like someone had lifted a veil. I had scored!! Oblivious to external things, I think I heard, "Take your helmet off!" This wasn't easy! After struggling for what seemed forever, I managed to get it off. As I waved to the crowd, someone told me to go to midfield. Then I was aware of applause, and I heard the announcer say something. I turned toward my team and gave the high sign. My last run to glory came during the 2000 Black and White Scrimmage. We were celebrating Leonard George's retirement as Athletic Director. The announcer was speaking about my retirement after 27 years of service with Spring I.S.D. I had taught and coached 37 years and it had been more than 40 years since I had even had a uniform on, much less score a touchdown! My "last run to glory" was terrific. I want to thank all of the football coaches at Spring High school, the entire staff, and the entire great group of Spring players that opened up the holes and let me slip through. The kind group of Spring defenders had well-rehearsed their best "Houston-Buffalo game" tackling. It was indeed a great thrill for me, as well as an honor and a privilege. The trainers were outstanding in getting me equipped and supplying me with a Doak Walker # 37. My "last run to glory" was a complete and thrilling experience. There is nothing like a touchdown to exhilarate you. Thanks for a great run!!

Footnote: Spring High head football coach, Sonny Karas, had approached me earlier in the week and asked if I would like to be involved in their spring Green and White scrimmage. He wanted to dress me in full uniform and run a trick play with me scoring. At 61 years old, I was capable of running pretty fast and one of my soccer players who also played football had told Coach Karas that I raced him his freshman year and won, so when Coach Karas considered this, he figured this would be a fun thing to do. On Friday we practiced what was going to happen and I was coached as to how to get the ball. The trick play required that I score from 50 yards out with lots of help from the defense and then I would be called to mid field where I would be honored. The trick play worked so well, most of the audience had no idea it was a trick play until I came to mid field and took off my helmet. Only then did they realize the one scoring the touchdown was **Don Henderson, retiring teacher.**

POSTSCRIPT 12/30/2022

When I first published this book and dedicated it to my good friend Eddie Nokes, he was still alive. Since that time, Eddie passed away (2017) and was interred in the Dallas/Ft. Worth Military cemetery in 2019. My wife and I attended this very moving ceremony, shared by family and friends.

Link to Eddie's Interment
https://howtotalktexun.com/2023/07/19/eddie-nokes-military-funeral/

Prior to Eddie's 2017 passing, several of the Southside and honorary members had passed away. The first was Royce who died in about 1972. His brother, Sammy passed away in the early 2000's and Gordon (Rooster) Lynne Dodson passed away in 2019. Remember our football games in the front yard when Sam Farrell was my Quarterback and Rooster was John Farrell's Quarterback. Sam passed away in 1999 and John in 2010. The members of the dynamite crew (except for me), are gone from this Earth. At this writing, P.D. Bankston is still with us. But several others have passed as well, including Billy Joe Robertson, Donnie Robertson, Stanley (Red) Johnson and perhaps others I have forgotten. Often, I pick up this book and re-read a few of our adventures and relive those days again.

ANOTHER FINE MESS YOU GOT ME IN, ROYCE!!

H. I. G. H.

He's In God's Hands

By Don Henderson 1/16/19

He's in God's Hands
No longer an Earthly Man
Fought he this life and
All its Strife

No more battle of Earth's
Physical ills
No more facing Death
And Earthly Chills

In God's hands he now lies
Leaving behind his
Earthly ties

Yes, we'll miss him and
Always shall,
God granted us the privilege of
Leaving us Memories we can tell

So long, Dear Friend
Thank you for being "You"
You being "You" is why we will
Miss "You"

Thank you, God, for protecting us all those years from ourselves.

Please go to Amazon and write a review for: "My W.C. Fields"/ "My Walnut Creek and the Southside Gang"

Albert D. Henderson's "Other Books":

- "The Return of How to Talk Texan",
- "Growing up in Grandmother's Beauty Shop", and
- "Diary of a Backwoods Preacher"

Printed in Great Britain
by Amazon